PRAISE FOR JOY SEEKER

"Shannon Kaiser is an incredible woman on a mission to help people find peace, happiness, and fulfillment in their lives. Her desire to serve others shines through all of her work."
—GABRIELLE BERNSTEIN, #1 *New York Times* bestselling author of *The Universe Has Your Back*

"One of the freshest voices in mental health and wellness, Shannon is on a mission to empower others to be true to themselves and live their full potential."
—MARCI SHIMOFF, *New York Times* bestselling author of *Happy for No Reason* and *Chicken Soup for the Woman's Soul*

"I admire Shannon because she's battled her own demons and has emerged with an enthusiasm for life, a belief in herself, and a passion for helping others identify and pursue what they truly want."
—LORI DESCHENE, founder of TinyBuddha.com and author of *Tiny Buddha: Simple Wisdom for Life's Hard Questions*

"Who couldn't use some more joy in their life? Shannon is an expert in all things happiness, and this guidebook shows us what's possible when we remove fear and choose love."
—EMMA LOEWE, sustainability editor at mindbodygreen and co-author of *The Spirit Almanac: A Modern Guide to Ancient Self-Care*

"*Joy Seeker* will transport the reader into a fascinating inner and outer journey, an unforgettable adventure of self-discovery, wonder, and awe."
—REBECCA CAMPBELL, bestselling author of *Light Is the New Black* and *Rise Sister Rise*

"In a culture of burnout and distraction, Shannon transports you into a world of wonder and joy, where you'll transcend the trappings of a fearful mind to access your truest self. If you've been searching for your authentic path, consider this your guide."

—AMBER RAE, bestselling author of *Choose Wonder Over Worry*

"When you get serious about seeking joy, everything starts to shift. This warm and uplifting book shows a clear path to discovering exactly where joy is for you—both as you are now and for who you are becoming."

—SARA WISEMAN, author of *Messages from the Divine: Wisdom for the Seeker's Soul*

"Shannon is a true joy seeker, showing us how to let go of what no longer works for us and lead an authentic life."

—AMY B. SCHER, energy therapist and bestselling author of *How to Heal Yourself When No One Else Can*

"*Joy Seeker* is not just another feel-good book to graze over. Instead, you will get a deep dive into your own reasons for being. This is the road map to authentic living and Shannon teaches you how to be the hero of your own life."

—BARBARA STANNY HUSON, author of *Sacred Success: A Course in Financial Miracles*

"Now more than ever, we as women need to rise up and empower ourselves and each other. Shannon's book is the necessary guidebook we need to get ourselves there."

—ANDREA OWEN, author of *How to Stop Feeling Like Sh*t: 14 Habits That Are Holding You Back from Happiness*

"Shannon gives you an easy-to-follow road map to lasting happiness, joy, and inner transformation. People say happiness is an inside job—this is the ultimate how-to manual."
> —AMY LEIGH MERCREE, bestselling author of *The Mood Book*

"Shannon's blazing one helluva self-love trail for others to show up, release fear, and live life fully. You know, one where our dreams come true and we live happily ever after, in love—with ourselves! The world needs this joy injection. And so do you."
> —EMMA MILDON, bestselling author of *The Soul Searcher's Handbook* and *Evolution of Goddess*

"Shannon is an absolute Goddess. She's a beautiful example of what is possible when you free yourself from self-criticism, blame, and guilt, and choose love instead. I am in total adoration of this woman, and that's because of how in love she is with herself, the world, and life! Thank you. Readers, you are in for a treat!"
> —MEL WELLS, bestselling author of *Hungry for More: Satisfy Your Deepest Cravings, Feed Your Dreams, and Live a Full-Up Life*

"Shannon offers easy-to-absorb advice to help you become your happiest, most-loved, highest-potential self—and best of all she makes it a fun process. My kind of gal."
> —KAREN SALMANSOHN, bestselling author of *How to Be Happy, Dammit: A Cynic's Guide to Spiritual Happiness*

OTHER BOOKS BY SHANNON KAISER

*The Self-Love Experiment: Fifteen Principles for
Becoming More Kind, Compassionate, and Accepting
of Yourself*

*Adventures for Your Soul: 21 Ways to Transform
Your Habits and Reach Your Full Potential*

*Find Your Happy Daily Mantras: 365 Days of
Motivation for a Happy, Peaceful and Fulfilling Life
(with card deck)*

*Find Your Happy: An Inspirational Guide to Loving
Life to Its Fullest*

ONLINE COURSES

*How to Find Your Calling & Live a Life with More
Meaning* (MindBodyGreen Video Course)

The Self-Love Home Retreat
www.playwiththeworld.com

JOY SEEKER

**LET GO OF WHAT'S HOLDING YOU BACK
SO YOU CAN LIVE THE LIFE YOU
WERE MADE FOR**

Shannon Kaiser

CITADEL PRESS
Kensington Publishing Corp.
www.kensingtonbooks.com

CITADEL PRESS BOOKS are published by

Kensington Publishing Corp.
119 West 40th Street
New York, NY 10018

All Kensington titles, imprints, and distributed lines are available at special quantity discounts for bulk purchases for sales promotions, premiums, fundraising, educational, or institutional use. Special book excerpts or customized printings can also be created to fit specific needs. For details, write or phone the office of the Kensington sales manager: Kensington Publishing Corp., 119 West 40th Street, New York, NY 10018, attn: Sales Department; phone 1-800-221-2647.

CITADEL PRESS and the Citadel logo are Reg. U.S. Pat. & TM Off.

ISBN-13: 978-0-8065-4025-2
ISBN-10: 0-8065-4025-7

First trade paperback printing: November 2019

10 9 8 7 6 5 4 3 2 1

Printed in the United States of America

Electronic edition:

ISBN-13: 978-0-8065-4026-9 (e-book)
ISBN-10: 0-8065-4026-5 (e-book)

To Denise Silvestro
Thank you for your passion
for this project and all my work.
I love our partnership and you.

And Summer Bacon and Dr. Peebles:
Thank you for your continued support
and unwavering guidance.
I love you.

Contents

PART 2: THE RELEASING
*(How to Let Go of Thinking
It Needs to Be Different)*

PART 3: THE BECOMING
*(How to Embrace What Is
While Creating What Could Be)*

PART 8: THE BEING
(How to Be Happy with Your Extraordinary, Somewhat Ordinary Life)

*Make the most of your Joy Seeker Journey
and download the Joy Seeker audio
meditation for FREE here:*

www.playwiththeworld.com/joyseekermeditation

One who
is connected
to their
True Self
is more powerful
than millions
who are not.

#JoySeeker

Welcome, Joy Seeker

THERE IS AN ENORMOUS AMOUNT of pressure, fear, and frustration on the planet right now. People feel overwhelmed and hopeless. We are fatigued, emotionally drained, and concerned for the well-being of the planet, our loved ones, and ourselves. Fear, judgment, and a lack of faith are at an all-time high, and they seem to be dictating our lives. For so many of us, we've lost the capacity to find our joy and see any real magic in being alive.

When this happens the tendency is to retreat. So many of us shut down emotionally, physically, even spiritually. We become a shell of who we really are. We drop into survival mode and do everything we can to just make it through the day, all while fear is driving our focus. But what if there was another way . . .

What if instead of falling into fear, we leaned into love?
What if instead of listening to our head, we believed in our heart?
What if instead of retreating inward, we expanded outward?
What if instead of shutting down, we opened up?

What if instead of ignoring our own needs, we honored
     them?

What if instead of fearing life, we began to trust it?

What if instead of obsessing about the past or future,
     we lived so fully in the present that nothing else
     mattered?

What if instead of feeling drained, exhausted, and
     overwhelmed, we felt excited, passionate, and
     purposeful?

What if instead of chasing happiness, we allowed joy?

This way of life is possible. It is the only way to heal ourselves and transform the world. Welcome to the Joy Seeker Journey.

This book is a gift to you. Your true self led you here.

This process is about you, and letting yourself be seen, heard, and felt in ways that you've yet to do. And that means by the world, and by your true self.

This is a journey about love, passion, desire, and authenticity. It will show you all the ways in which you hide from yourself and the world, and gently crack you open in a nurturing, harmonious process to help you see your own light and be unapologetic about shining it.

The journey will show you the pieces of you that want to be held, looked at, probed, and recognized. It will remind you that you are never alone, and that there is great love within you and all around you. This path forward is about connecting to the greatest love of your entire life, the true self within.

This book will give you the opportunity to reveal to yourself your deepest truth, the reason you are here, the core of your being, your light in the world. Like any grand journey, the path you are about to embark on is full of surprises, insights, excitement, and wonder. Keep an open heart and mind and your journey will transform you. This book will remind you that like everything in the world, you can be reborn—but not from a place of lack, for you will soon see your grandness.

As you travel through the world and journey deeper into who you truly are, you will be more present. You will learn what joy truly means to you. You will go deep within yourself to discover the layers of you that have been longing to be expressed. You will learn what matters most in the entire world to you, and joyfully create a life to align with your core values.

This is the promise of the Joy Seeker Journey.

How to Get the Most out of This Book

This book is designed to maximize your potential by helping you connect to your true self. There are many resources throughout the process to support you on your journey. I've listed them here.

Joy Journal

Throughout the book and at the end of each section will be important questions and journal prompts. Because the Joy Seeking Journey will suggest journaling exercises from the get-go, I invite you to get a journal specifically for this process.

You can invest in a fancy one or a simple spiral notebook. The goal is to treat this like a project and quest. It's best to get a journal to accompany the process and do all the exercises suggested, so you can track and celebrate your journey.

Joy Jaunts

Throughout the book you will see pullout sections called Joy Jaunts. A *jaunt* is a short excursion or journey made for pleasure and deeper insight. The exercises are designed to help you connect to your authentic self and get out of your comfort zone. Each exercise is strategically matched to the section you are studying. Some may seem odd, silly, or even pointless, but I promise you everything is connected and designed to maximize your potential. Give yourself permission to try them out and explore all tools presented in the book.

Free I Am Joy Meditation

I created a powerful meditation to help you return to joy and connect to your truth, which is love and inner peace. Whenever you feel overwhelmed, stressed, anxious, or simply want to maintain a positive attitude, this quick guided meditation can help. The digital download is available for free here: www.playwiththeworld.com/joyseekermeditation.

More Resources

At the end of the book I've listed my favorite books that helped me along my own path to self-actualization and inner peace. They can help you take this work deeper and continue on your own joy seeking journey.

Daily Support and Guidance

If you are looking for daily support, you can join my uplifting online community and connect with like-minded people or work with me in private or group coaching.

Facebook: @ShannonKaiserWrites
Instagram: @ShannonKaiserWrites
Website: www.playwiththeworld.com
Coaching: www.playwiththeworld.com/work-with-me/

It is my greatest hope that you dive into this process like a child full of wonder. Explore the layers of yourself and your life and you will soon see that you are not off track, you are never behind, and you are actually exactly where you are supposed to be. Everything is always in perfect order when you are the Joy Seeker.

Welcome to the most extraordinary, seemingly ordinary, adventure of your life.

It starts right here, the moment you turn the page. You are choosing to connect to your
true self and live a life with massive meaning.

Welcome to the true you, Joy Seeker.

Your future self has been waiting.

THE World NEEDS YOU AND YOUR Joy

#JoySeeker

I wish I'd Had
the Courage to live
a life true to myself
not the life others
expected of me...

#JoySeeker

Introduction

THE JOY SEEKER WAY

*I*T SEEMS TO ME OUR lives can be sectioned off into moments. Pivotal moments that redirect us, force us to go inward, and remind us what it really means to be alive. There's a pivotal moment in my life that got me to this point right here. Our pivotal moments help define our direction and, if we are willing, they can be our greatest teachers. This book is a result of me coming face-to-face with what matters most and really going inward to decide, what does joy truly mean?

My Joy Seeker Journey actually began on the saddest day of my life, which was my pivotal moment. It was October 13, 2017, and I had to say good-bye to my best friend, Tucker, a golden retriever rescue who had come into my world eight years earlier and transformed me and my life in so many ways. With Tucker by my side and his unconditional love, I went from being clinically depressed to anxiety free and learning how to love myself, be myself, and live a life with joy. Tucker had been aging, his body slowing down, and for months I wondered if each day would be the last with my beautiful boy. Holding him in my arms when his soul left his body was both agonizing and one of the most beautiful experiences I had ever witnessed. It was profound because I knew there was great love between us. I had given myself permission to love deeply and feel immense joy. But in this moment of him passing, my joy was escaping me, too. I realized that Tucker, in the way I knew him, was gone forever, but a warm presence wrapped around me and I felt it was Tucker telling me it would be okay. But it didn't feel okay; a part of my spirit died along with him. How could I exist without my joy?

Ironically, or maybe not, it was my grief that guided me forward, teaching me how to show up even more fully for myself and my life. *Who do you want to be in the world? Who are you really?* These questions circled around in my head, and I realized that it was time for me to grow beyond what I had known before. I had to learn how to find joy and commit to happiness without relying on anything or anyone else. This realization led to the most extraordinary journey of my life. You see, I didn't know it at the time, but losing the thing I loved more than life itself made me fight for my own life. For the next several months, I went on a deep, inward search to find out who I really was. To find out what matters most to me and what my life is really about. I went on my own Joy Seeker Journey.

You may be wondering, what is the Joy Seeker Journey? The big picture: It is a process for understanding your life and the balance of everything in it. It is the blueprint, the foundation, for you to be who you really are and live out your true calling. Each one of us has a divine purpose, a soul mission, and a personal plan, and the Joy Seeker Journey is your own undertaking into the life you're meant to live. It's about you having the courage to show up more fully in the world and shine your bright, gorgeous, natural light.

The seed of an idea started to sprout when I read a study that said the most common regrets of the dying are, "I wish I'd had the courage to live a life true to myself, not the life others expected of me" and "I wish that I had let myself be happier." When I read that, it changed everything for me. At that point in my life, I was comfortable in my career. I was happy and felt self-love, but something was still a little off. It was only after Tucker died and I was forced to find a source of joy within myself that I realized the thing that was missing was my fullest expression of self-actualization; I wasn't yet living my life to its full potential. That study revealed that most of us are alive, but not really living. I could see with my life coaching clients and from people around the world who attended my workshops that most of us are struggling. It's the painful struggle that comes with stumbling through life wondering if this is all there is. We feel stuck and off track, thinking we are behind or it is supposed to look and feel different than it does.

Struggling, feeling stuck in life is what we know. Although we would never admit it, struggle is comfortable to many of us because we think that is how it is supposed to be. Our parents struggled, just as their parents did before them. So part of us identifies with the struggle that keeps us stuck and we play it safe and stay static because it's easy. But the truth is, it's much easier to be happy and joyful than it is to be stuck. We just need to learn how to liberate ourselves and let joy become our default.

So how do we do it? How do we find our way out? This is where the Joy Seeker approach to life can help us. When we are stuck in our struggle, we don't have clarity. We can't move forward, mainly because we aren't sure what forward looks like. But through the Joy Seeker process you will recognize that the "stuckness" can birth new opportunity. Your struggle can help steer you in the direction of understanding, and this will lead to a deeper connection to your true self. When you look within, you will discover your authentic truth, and the expression of this truth is the greatest gift you can give to yourself and to the world.

Your happiness, your health, and your authenticity are the golden tickets to freedom and feeling peace within. And the good news is, you don't have to do, change, or become anything. All you need to do is be more you. It's a process of less doing and more being. You can release the struggle, let go of the worry, and detach from the drama and stress. This journey we are about to embark on together will give you permission to experience more joy, love, and light. You deserve it and you are worth it.

The majority of our Joy Seeker Journey will be about you discovering who you really are so you can be true to yourself. This is a book about clarity, purpose, and passion, a process for authentic living. It's about knowing you are safe to express the true you. In fact, you showing up more fully is how you can help to transform the entire world.

"Don't ask what the world needs. Ask what makes you come alive, and go do it. Because what the world needs is people who have come alive."
—Howard Thurman

Feeling dissatisfied with your life is a signal that you are made for more. I spent much of my life thinking something was wrong with me because I couldn't just be comfortable and satisfied. Whether I was uncomfortable in my body or feeling out of place in life, something was always "off." No matter what new goal I achieved, it was never enough and I never felt good enough. But all of that changed when I dived headfirst into my own Joy Seeker Journey.

So many of us are looking for happiness outside of ourselves. I did for decades, and it resulted in clinical depression, anxiety, addictions, and eating disorders. Even when Tucker entered my life and brought me joy, it still was an external source. It wasn't until he was physically gone that I was forced to look within. And I asked myself a question that changed everything. I asked, "What have you always wanted to do but haven't given yourself permission to do?" And in that moment, like a racehorse out of the gate, my inner voice said, *travel the world for an entire year.* Then I asked myself, *Why am I not doing that?* As a writer, life coach, and speaker, I can work from anywhere in the world. Why was I putting my dreams on hold? Did my life need to look a certain way before I could live out my ideal life? The only thing holding me back was fear of the unknown and excuses I told myself that kept me playing small. So I sat down and pulled out my pen and paper. I started to create my ideal vision—my own yearlong journey. And just like that I made the shift from talking about it to actually doing something about it. So often we talk about wanting to change, we think about it and say we will do it, but year after year, nothing really changes. The truth is, nothing will ever change until you decide to make it happen.

But here's the thing, we all think we want change, but change is scary and it doesn't last. We can change back.

> *"And the day came when the risk to remain tight in a bud was more painful than the risk it took to blossom."*
>
> —Anaïs Nin

This is why diets don't work, and we go back to the relationships or jobs that sucked the life out of us. As psychotherapist Terri Cole says, "What we really crave is transformation." Because when you transform you become everything you always knew you could be and you are living your highest potential—you are fully actualized. It's as if someone has turned on the light and you can suddenly see so clearly that your newfound clarity lights up your world. Yes, that is where we are heading, to full self-actualization and shiny bright lights. That is the Joy Seeker way.

For so long, I thought joy would come from achievements, from setting out to check as many things as possible off my bucket list. Living a fulfilling life meant actualizing my dreams, but as you will soon see, this journey is so much more than that.

My Joy Seeker Journey started as a one-year journey around the globe. This is a dream that I've held dear for over two decades, and I assumed making it into a reality would bring me incredible joy and fulfillment—which it did, but not in the way you would imagine. And that is the gift of this journey: You may not get what you think you want, but you will always get what you truly need.

This is not an outward journey you are about to embark on. It is an inward quest to discover your true self so you can actualize your highest potential in the world.

This method will give you a deeper understanding of who you are and help you gain the courage to live out your highest potential. Living a life pursuing, following, and actualizing your dreams is part of living a joyful life, but we will go so much deeper than just what you want.

Most likely there's some part of your life that feels a little lifeless, and you know it could be so much better, but you aren't quite sure how. Maybe you've found your soul mate, and have more money than you know what to do with, but you feel stuck in a soul-suffocating career. Maybe you are connected to your purpose and are blissfully sharing your talent and gifts with the world, but you have no idea how you are going to pay your next bill.

Fulfillment and happiness don't come from stuff or things we collect but rather they exist in the process of creating and being true to ourselves.

Maybe you are passionately pursuing your dreams, yet with each new goal and achievement, you feel just as empty and disconnected as ever. Maybe you look like you have it all together, but you cry yourself to sleep each night. Or maybe you are living the life you want, but for some reason you still don't feel fulfilled. This process will reveal to you the truth of who you are, and identify why, as a culture, a society, and as individuals, we feel so off. So many of us we think we are problems that can't be solved, we are saturated in our own stuckness and wonder why everyone else seems so happy, healthy, and together. We want control of what we can't seem to grasp, our anxiety fuels our daily actions, and we have forgotten about joy. After all, we are just trying to make it through the day in one piece. But that is exactly the point: We have forgotten about joy, and joy misses us. Joy wants to be part of our life. This is an invitation for you to connect with who you truly are, which is love, which is joy, which is light.

You may be thinking, *Okay, lady, that's all well and good, but can't you just tell me how to get unstuck? How do I find my happy? CliffsNotes please, I want the magic bullet! How to get from where I am to where I want to be? Help me now!* I know this feeling so deeply because I, too, used to think I wanted the answers, anything to pull me out of my stuckness. I was like a junkie—give me the quick fix to numb me from my overwhelming sadness: sugar, shopping, sex, sleeping, binge-watching, anything to help me avoid the sinking sensation that I felt off track and behind in life. Why did everyone else seem to have it together? I thought. Why was joy escaping me? Why couldn't I just be happy and accept where I was?

I wanted desperately to know the one way that would fix me, change me, help me get out of my own static routine, but what I've learned and what you will soon see is that this isn't a quick fix; it's a process, a journey. Not some painful, excruciating, drawn-out, "uphill in ten feet of snow both ways" type of journey, but rather an uplifting and inspiring journey of excitement, wonder, and awe. Because in this quest you get to become your own hero. You will rise up and slay all the emotional dragons, which look like expectations, demands, pressure, stress, anxiety, and guilt, so you can be free to fly effortlessly above all the drama and connect to unlimited joy and inner peace.

Make a pact with yourself to treat your life, and this process, like an expedition, an explorer's journey, a project, even an experiment. When we can approach our life and goals this way, we will be able to feel joy more freely. Why? Because we are not so wrapped up in the destination. Instead we relax into the journey and that is where true joy lives, in the process of being instead of doing. You are now working on the journey to your true self. The path you are about to embark on will help you:

- Free yourself from outside pressure, stress, anxiety, and worry
- Know on a soul level why you are here and what you are meant to do
- Give up the need to please others, change yourself, or be different so you can accept yourself whole-heartedly
- Understand that you always fit in the world, even when it tries to make you feel like you don't
- Gain the insight and clarity to have the courage to be true to yourself
- Learn how to live a life that feels meaningful and rewarding to you on a soul level
- Feel unlimited joy no matter what is happening in your life or what you are doing
- Discover an unshakable inner peace that you never imagined existed
- Give yourself permission to be you in all your gorgeous glory
- Replace judgment, comparison, and anxiety with compassion, kindness, and love
- Learn how to stop chasing, controlling, waiting, or hoping for happiness and discover it within

This book is a how-to guide, and as you go through each part, you will see how it all works together. Each part represents a phase or part of your journey. It is a rite of passage for us to go through each part, but we don't always realize we are going through phases. If you begin to look at your life in this manner, as parts (like a part to a play or movie), it will not only help you feel more peace in the journey but relax and release the pressure to have it be different. When we are relaxed, we can get more guidance versus being tense, trying to control the outcome, and closed off. Keep an open mind and this process will be so much more fun for you. Because let's face it, we all would like some instant relief. We want relief from the world, the one that tries to tell us to be different than we are, buy more, do more, reach for more in order to be happy. We need relief from the expectations, demands, and the daily stresses. We need relief from the false versions of ourselves. Can we just hit stop? Can we quiet that little, mean voice that tells us that no matter how much work we've done, how hard we try, how far we've come, how good of a person, mother, coworker, others tell us we are, we still aren't enough, and we're not where we should be? Chances are, if you're reading this, something feels off. You may not be able to put your finger on it, and that's okay—because it doesn't matter if your off is rock bottom, crying hysterically on the bathroom floor (I've been there), or if your off looks like feeling pretty good, content, but not sure why you can't feel even better (welcome to the club)—the point is, you are not alone and this book is for you.

It doesn't matter where you are in your journey, because where you are is exactly where you need to be to get to where you want to go.

⌒

So for starters let's pinky-promise to be more compassionate, kind, and gentle with ourselves. The journey we are about to embark on will be so much more fulfilling if you can tell your inner critic to chill the freak out. The more open you can be throughout this entire process, the more joy you will feel and the faster you will be able to connect to your true self.

Although my ultimate joy is traveling, this is not a travel book nor is it my own memoir of my trip around the world, but rather this is the process it takes to live your highest form of joy, which I did while traveling full time. This is a guidebook to not only help you gain massive clarity but have the courage to follow through on your heart's desires so you can truly connect to your true self.

At the core, it is about connecting to your heart and giving yourself the permission to live a life that is true to yourself on every level.

In the book *This School Called Planet Earth*, Summer Bacon talks about our life being a creative adventure, and that means creation is the most essential part of living. When we aren't creating, a piece of us feels trapped, stuck, frustrated. I don't just mean creating in the sense of painting, writing, or being an artist (although if that's what you love, then make sure to keep doing it). Creating can also be working on self-care, showing up for yourself, having a great deep conversation with a friend, being present in the unfolding journey, focusing on your goals, and living your life with more meaning. Creating is living—to be alive is to be a creator. When we feel bored, frustrated, or off, it's often because we've stopped creating, we've stopped expressing ourselves. We've lost the humanity. From here on out, look at yourself and life as if you are the artist of your own masterpiece. You get to decide what you want on your canvas. Consider the paint you use as the inspiration that comes to you. When you are inspired, trust it.

Your life is your masterpiece. But the masterpiece doesn't just happen overnight. It is a creative process. For example, I wasn't able to write this book until I stepped fully into my own potential by following my heart to live overseas, and in doing that everything became richer, more fulfilling, and clearer. I found what I was looking for: fulfillment, joy, purpose, and connection.

So why should you become a Joy Seeker? Simply put, you deserve to be enchanted, stunned, even impressed by life. We want to live outside the lines and color our canvases so bright that we light up our life and feel inspired from within. Because living outside the lines is where massive growth happens.

You are ready to make the most of your own life, or else you wouldn't have picked up this book. Welcome to the Joy Seeker Journey. It is a way of life, where we commit to growth because that is where true joy lives. As we learn more about ourselves and more about our place in this world, we start to see life in a new way. Things become easier and we become an example of what is possible. When we truly know ourselves, we can love and express ourselves openly, and this is the highest form of satisfaction there is.

Joy Seeking is about self-expression. It is about living in complete accordance with who you are at a soul level.

To be a Joy Seeker is about trusting in yourself and the Universe and honoring your soul's true calling. This isn't something that is reserved for the few. Every one of us can opt into a life that makes us feel good. Becoming a Joy Seeker means you commit to living a life that feels good on the inside, which will manifest on the outside.

It is a process we undergo that allows us to be more real and authentic in our experience of life. It's the stripping away of all the nonsense, the superficial, the things that don't align with our truth, the things that don't resonate or make us feel good. I am here to help you connect to your authentic joy, which in essence is your true self. But I can't do that if I am not living, breathing, and expressing my joy first and foremost for me, which is why I've dedicated the past few years to being a full-time Joy Seeker, to be able to share the power of this work and way of living firsthand.

Being true to yourself is the highest form of happiness and fulfillment.

This is a gift to yourself because you will finally be able to say, "I am worth it. I deserve more. I am proud to be me." I know why you are here reading this. It is the same reason I set out to travel for a full year. It is the same reason I wrote this book. You want something you don't currently have in your life, more joy.

But first realize that joy is different for all of us. What brings me joy is not your recipe for everlasting happiness. Think about it, for Da Vinci, it was understanding the ways of the Universe, for Monet it was nature and color, for Robin Williams it was connection and laughter, and Anthony Bourdain it was travel and food. True joy is so much deeper than just one thing. For all of us, joy is in the experience, the expression, how it makes us feel. Joy is a profound sense of physical, emotional, and spiritual connection and well-being.

What brings you joy? That's what you're going to discover on this amazing journey.

This process is designed to give you the courage to be who you are meant to be so you can connect more deeply to yourself and everything and everyone around you.

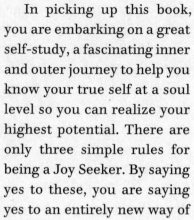

In picking up this book, you are embarking on a great self-study, a fascinating inner and outer journey to help you know your true self at a soul level so you can realize your highest potential. There are only three simple rules for being a Joy Seeker. By saying yes to these, you are saying yes to an entirely new way of life. One that feels good from the inside out, one that makes you feel alive, connected, and in constant joy.

The Joy Seeker Way

1. Let go of all expectations and be fully in the journey.
2. Trust ourselves and life more fully and live openly from our heart.
3. See our life as an unfolding creative adventure.

Are you ready to join me?
Let's commit to being Joy Seekers.
Because the world needs you and your joy.
Let's begin.

the Joy Seeker Way

1. LET GO OF ALL EXPECTATIONS AND BE FULLY IN THE JOURNEY.

2. TRUST OURSELVES AND LIFE MORE FULLY AND LIVE OPENLY FROM OUR HEART.

3. SEE OUR LIFE AS AN UNFOLDING CREATIVE ADVENTURE.

#JoySeeker

Joy
SAT ME DOWN
AND SAID

"It's time to talk...
I've missed you."

#JoySeeker

PART 1

THE REALIZING

**How to Identify the Barriers
Blocking You from Bliss**

Where's My Joy?

LET GO OF DISTRACTIONS, A.K.A. ENERGY SUCKERS

Serious transformations begin with two commitments: The courage to try new things and act in new ways, and the honesty needed to no longer hide from or lie to ourselves.

—YUNG PUEBLO

I'M SCRAPING THE BOTTOM OF the Ben & Jerry's pint of ice cream, and Netflix just asked, "Are you still watching," which means my binge night is perhaps slightly out of control. It's a Friday night, only 7:30 p.m., and I'm in my pj's. A typical situation for me. It's been several months since Tucker passed on. It's raining outside, which somehow makes me feel like my hibernation is warranted.

I know you're thinking one of two things: *Girl, you're a self-help author who writes about being happy. That doesn't sound very self-helpy.* Or maybe, just maybe, you feel me. You are me. *I get it! Seriously, sometimes life is hard.* Only maybe it's not Ben & Jerry's. Maybe your fingers are slapping the bottom of the potato chip bag. Or perhaps food isn't even your escape, but there's something in your life that is off. You feel stuck, disconnected, even unsure. Maybe you're not curled up on your couch at all, but instead you're keeping yourself so busy, filling up your entire calendar, jam-packed so you don't have any downtime, you don't let yourself feel the uneasiness bubbling within.

Running from my feelings, this was my reality for as long as I could recall. True happiness was always just outside my reach. For me, my escape into bottomless pits of creamy sugar and milk accompanied by Hallmark movies on repeat was my way of coping with what was uncomfortable to admit: "I feel off track and behind in life. I don't feel like I'm where I'm supposed to be."

You see at that point in my life, I was consumed with "getting there." "There" is the elusive place that we think happiness exists in. It's the next thing, the bigger house, the better place, the new job title, the soul mate, the lottery win, the trip around the world. It doesn't necessarily matter what "there" is because we are convinced it is where our happiness lives. And as long as we are "here," we can't be "there," so we convince ourselves we can't be satisfied, we can't find the joy.

We get stuck in an eternal state of reaching for the elusive "there," and many of us turn to habits, addictions, mindless activities like overworking, or keeping ourselves so busy we don't have to feel the uneasiness. I lived this way for so many years that I didn't even realize my anxiety was running the show. Most of us are looking for happiness outside of ourselves. We genuinely believe if we could just get that raise, that new car, hit our goal weight, get that new outfit, new home, new job title, new relationship, and so on, then our life would be better.

We stay stuck and unhappy because we don't realize that chasing happiness will never actually bring it to us.

You can imagine with this mentality, the enormous pressure I put on myself to be more, have more, do more, and get more. I was trapped in an invisible race with a nonexistent version of myself—that was always just outside my reach. The worst part was that this version was inauthentic. I wasn't necessarily chasing after things I wanted; I was running after things I was told I should want. I was doing what the world, society, family expected of me, but not necessarily what I wanted of myself.

It's easy to think something is wrong with us if we don't "measure up" to the ideals the world imposes upon us, and we don't ever stop to question the world. We allow it to make us feel less than and unworthy. I used to suffer from depression and eating disorders in part because I thought something was wrong with me. I'd look at photo-shopped magazine covers and think I paled in comparison. I'd hear stories of others' success and accomplishments and think I'd never be that good. The problem isn't all these things in the world that make us feel bad, but the power we give to things outside of ourselves. We allow ourselves to become disconnected from our true selves and let the world guide us, instead of our heart and inner compass.

The change for me was when I stopped trusting the world and instead turned inward to trust myself.

Naturally if we want to start feeling better, we need to reconnect with our true selves and reclaim our power. A good place to start is to be more conscious of the messages we allow to infiltrate our minds. We need to stop giving our power to others. We can shut out judgment, comparison, and negativity. As long as you are looking outward to the media, pop culture, friends' advice, other people's views, you can't look inward. The fix is to reclaim your power and disconnect from all the things outside of yourself draining your energy, frustrating you, or causing you to worry. We do this by learning how to trust ourselves. When we feel more secure in our own beliefs, we operate, not from a place of fear, but grounded in love. Ask yourself, Where are you giving your power away? What is draining your energy? In today's fractured world, it can be difficult to operate from a place of love, but now more than ever, it is absolutely essential. I looked at my own life and saw that fear and worry were keeping me stuck. I was also holding on to anger and frustration. I was giving a lot of focus to things that were draining me. I would think about the past, obsess about the future, worry about uncertain outcomes.

I knew if I wanted to feel better I would have to eliminate distractions and things draining my energy. First, I started by looking at my information consumption and mindless screen time. I unfollowed social media accounts that didn't make me feel joy. I started following more positive news sites, and I started to send love energetically to everyone. Yes, you read that correctly: I sent love to all the people, even the people I didn't understand, even the ones whose values I didn't share. The exes that hurt me? I prayed for them; I wished wellness for all humanity. Because spreading this love and light not only took me out of negativity and hate, it helped bring more joy into my world. It may sound crazy, but if you can send love through prayer, meditation, or just kind thoughts to all people and situations—especially the ones you dislike and don't understand—you will feel more grounded within yourself. You will also welcome more love into your life, and this is the catalyst for everything. Your true self does not want to judge or hate or condemn. Your real self is love and wants to spread this love to others. Think about if someone or something is energetically taking up a lot of your focus. Are you mad at someone or having a hard time forgiving? When we send negative thoughts and hate to others, we are taking ourselves outside of our own potential. We limit our own capacity for healing by leaning into negativity. One of my favorite music artists, Matt Nathanson, said at his concert recently that just because someone has different opinions, points of view, and beliefs doesn't make them any less human. Instead of separating because of our differences, we can come together in our humanity.

Imagine yourself for a moment like an octopus, with tentacles reaching out, and each bad experience and pain from your past is attached to one of those tentacles. Each person you don't like—your boss, a politician, your neighbor, your mother who didn't support you, your best friend from high school who betrayed you, your sibling who screwed the family, the ex who you still don't have closure with, and so forth—is attached to a tentacle. And your energy is being sucked out of you to all of them, draining you. Furthermore, you are stretched out and spread super thin. Holding on to resentments can even cause physical pain.

One of the easiest ways for us to return to our joy is to bring our power back by not holding anger toward others. Stop judging others for the way they do things and instead try to see the bigger picture. Everyone is doing the best they can with what they know. If someone has done something you don't understand or they have wronged you, pray for them. Send them light. You don't want to be drained by the negative emotions. You don't want to stay stuck, mired in judgment and hate. Let compassion and love move you forward.

Who can you detach from energetically? Instead of holding anger, who can you forgive? Let go of the darkness and ground yourself in love.

Joy Jaunt: Media Detox

What is it you are consuming? I went on a media detox and unfollowed all social media accounts that didn't bring me joy. I went in to my email box and unsubscribed from any junk, spam, and accounts that cluttered up my life. Put yourself on your own media detox. Can you limit your news intake, start to question the source, lean into love instead of fear? Also, go to your social media accounts and only follow people who uplift you and make you feel inspired and connected to love. Do the same with your emails. Watch how your joy increases in direct proportion to your media decrease.

Here is a list of positive news sites to replace the negative ones with:

www.goodnewsnetwork.org
Founded by a former television producer, Good News
    Network (GNN) says its mission is to provide
    readers with a "daily dose of news to enthuse."

gimundo.com
Good news and positive stories are served up daily
    at Gimundo.

WHERE'S MY JOY — 33

aplus.com
Founded in 2014 by actor and technology investor,
Ashton Kutcher, A Plus covers the news criti-
cally, from all angles, but with hope.

thelightersidenetwork.com
A positive place to connect and grow your spirituality.

www.happynews.com
A team of citizen journalists report on positive, but
compelling, stories from around the world at
Happy News.

So many of us feel separated from society because we feel disconnected from ourselves.

By now it's probably clear that in order to overcome our fear and frustrations, we need to stop looking outside of ourselves. Plus we need to come together and celebrate our differences. Look at where you feel separated in your life. Where do you feel off track, behind, or on the outside looking in? As we dive deeper into this process you will see how much happier you will feel when you put down your guard, and instead of feeling defensive, scared, and worried, you lean into love and compassion. Once we bring our attention back to ourselves, and stop giving so much power away to outside forces, we have more energy to focus on what it is we truly need to feel like our true self.

Another reason we often feel stuck in life is because we feel disconnected. When we feel disconnected to our life, it is because we are being summoned to change. What we are living is no longer for our highest good. It is time to go inward and address our deepest needs.

That Friday night, sitting on the couch with my friends Ben & Jerry, something shifted. I looked down into my empty ice cream carton, and I knew the answers weren't at the bottom. It was time I roll up my sleeves and ask myself the real question that needed to be addressed. I looked around at my overpriced home and wondered, *Where's my joy?* When was the last time I did something just for fun, without expectations? When was the last time I truly felt inner peace and accepted where I was in life? When was the last time I felt deeply connected to all people and places? When was the last time I laughed so hard it hurt to breathe? And then the biggie... When was the last time I felt free of worry, anxiety, and fear?

I didn't like the answers, but I was finally on the right path. I decided to go a bit deeper. What was I doing instead of enjoying my life? Stuffing myself with ice cream? Burying myself in busyness? And why? We always have a choice. We can continue to let the world tell us how we should feel and fall into continued mindless escapism and disconnected joy, or we can click away from the habits that distract us and go deeper into our own life experience and find out what it is we are really missing. Instead of escaping my life, what if I started to ask why wasn't I actually enjoying it? Why did I think I needed to escape anyway?

The turning point for me was in the realization that the root of my discontentment was because I wasn't being true to myself. I wasn't asking myself the questions that lead to self-actualization. I wasn't listening to my own heart. At that time in my life, I thought there was seriously something wrong with me because I felt so stuck and bored. I often wondered why it was so hard to find joy, but in looking back, I now see that there was nothing wrong with me. I was just stuck in my worry. My worry was like a suit of armor I wore around me. It was part of my identity; I was attached to it. But by letting it define me I was hurting myself and those I loved because I wasn't expressing my true self. So many of us do this without even realizing it.

The first stage in our journey to connecting with our true self is to see where we've been giving our power away and then to understand that our stress, anxiety, and boredom in life have a profound purpose. Imagine that your frustrations in life are not happening to you but *for* you. Our worry is like an old relative, a seemingly unwelcomed guest, who pops up unannounced, but always has important, life-changing information to deliver. Instead of pushing it away or being annoyed that it showed up, we can allow it be our teacher.

Stress in any form always approaches us to guide us and show us a path to freedom. Instead of locking it out and pushing it away with mindless habits, can you invite it in? Ask it to dinner, take it with you and observe it, question it, be curious about your uneasiness. In seeking to understand why it is here, we can prevent it from consuming us. I started to see that my anxiety was like a young abandoned child in need of love. It wanted attention; it needed to be addressed and looked at and felt so that it could give me the lesson it came to deliver.

> *Once I stopped ignoring and avoiding my stress, I discovered that my anxiety wasn't trying to limit me, but free me from a life that no longer felt good.*

Once we embrace our discomforts, they can release their hold and no longer make a desperate attempt to get our attention. Often they settle and leave us with the gift of understanding as we grow and advance emotionally, mentally, and spiritually from their presence.

Many of us fall into a routine because it's comfortable, it helps us get by. But if we get honest, most of these routines aren't serving us. The routine is the habits that you do mindlessly keeping you from joy. For some, it's overeating, others overworking, overspending, rabbit-holing down YouTube or on social media, picking fights, avoiding, overanalyzing, stressing, worrying, escaping, and trying to do anything we can to convince others that things are better than we actually feel. Many of our habits happen on an unconscious or subconscious level and we're not fully aware of why we are doing them and fall into our routines automatically.

The key is to recognize the root of our habits. Become more aware that you may be operating on autopilot and start to question, observe, and analyze all the patterns that don't make you feel good. I was able to do this by observing my behaviors more critically, not from a place of judgment or shame, but out of curiosity. I got into the habit of asking myself, "Does this support the life I want to create?" This simple question helped me transform limited patterns and beliefs.

On the other side of these habits is where authentic joy lives. When we can understand what it is we are really trying to find (joy, peace, love) and what we've been running from (ourselves), we can release the anxiety and move toward what we really want.

What do you really want? Is what you are doing supporting the life you want to create? So many of us avoid the questions. I want to invite you, dear one, to befriend the questions. As you do, be patient with all that is unresolved within you. Try to love the questions themselves. For years I had so many questions, and not knowing the answers made me feel deficient, uneasy, even weak. As long as I was focusing on needing the answers, I stayed stuck in my own anxiety and guilt. Today, I don't run away from these inquires. I seek more questions; I collect them and dive into them. I let them dance around in my mind and drop softly into my heart. I've learned how to be comfortable in the unknown because as I probe deeper, I let the uncertainty be my compass forward. May you let the space in between lack of understanding and clarity motivate and inspire you instead of consuming you with worry and fear.

Ask them religiously, fearlessly, and dive into them head-first with reckless abandon. Throughout *Joy Seeker* there will be journal questions. These are the same questions I asked myself, and the ones I use in my private coaching practice to help people reach their potential. Don't skip over them. Take time to go inward and really ask yourself what you've needed to learn. Those questions are your sanity, your lifeline—they will pull you forward. When we ask the soul-searching questions, honesty reveals itself. Commit to being more real with yourself. This is the path of the Joy Seeker and it will bring you freedom.

> *The questions we ask ourselves are our greatest allies in our quest to happiness.*

"What kind of life do I really want to live?" This was the big question that was looming over my every move, the one I was afraid to face. But once I did, instead of listening to the fear that lived in my head, I let my heart start to do the talking. We can make drastic changes inspired from our true self when we ask ourselves the important questions and listen to our heart.

Joy Jaunt: What Kind of Life Do You Want to Live?

Recognize that when we are anxious or off track, it's not something that needs to define us. It's simply our soul's calling begging us to be honest and recognize that who we are being in the world might not be serving us anymore. It's time to shed the layers and emerge into who you're meant to be. Pull out your joy journal and go deeper on these questions. They will help you connect to your authentic self.

Ask yourself:

- When do I feel like my best self?
- When do I feel the most alive?
- What brings me incredible joy?

We can move through the process by beginning the inner quest of discovering what it is we need most for fulfillment. Taking time to answer these questions will support you on your journey.

Radical Recap

JOY BUSTER (the thing that sabotages your joy): Energy suckers and distractions.

AWESOME OPPORTUNITY: Focus inward for your happiness.

MANTRA: "Everything I need is inside of me. I focus inward and align with my own brilliant light."

The Paris Syndrome

LET GO OF EXPECTATIONS

My happiness grows in direct proportion to my acceptance, and in inverse proportion to my expectations.

—MICHAEL J. FOX

I ASKED MYSELF WHAT IS it I'd always wanted to do, and "travel the world full-time" was my answer. So I set out on a great adventure and visited eighteen countries and twenty-eight cities. But in the beginning of my trip, as I arrived in each new location something interesting occurred: I kept feeling let down. I wasn't able to fully enjoy each place. It was the same feeling I experienced back home in America: Every time I reached my destination—whether that was a new job, a new personal goal, a new relationship—I was unfulfilled. That's when I realized that wherever we go, there we are. You can't run from who you are, and if there is a part of you that feels a specific way, like me not being able to be content with wherever I was, then that feeling will go with you wherever you are in the world. This is why we leave bad relationships only to find ourselves dating a similar person, or we leave jobs that suck the life out of us, only to be sitting in a new desk, with a new boss, but the same old feelings of uneasiness. There we go, but here we are.

During my travels, it occurred to me that my constant quest to reach happiness in the next best thing might have been a deeper issue. Why was it so hard for me to be happy with where I was? Even in the most beautiful places in the world, I had a difficult time appreciating it fully because I was always focused on the next thing. Is that why joy was always just outside my reach?

For as long as I could remember, all I ever thought about was traveling. But here I was traveling full-time, living my dream, and I couldn't fully enjoy it. Has something similar ever happened to you? Think about your own life and the pursuit of your goals. Have you ever gone after something only to be let down once you got it? Or were you immediately looking ahead to the next achievement, so you didn't even enjoy the one you just obtained? Truth be known, it is not uncommon for people to get something they dreamed of only to find it's not what they thought it would be. There is even a name for it: the Paris syndrome. The Paris syndrome, or *Syndrome de* Paris, is a real syndrome that affects travelers (mostly Japanese tourists to Paris). It is a transient mental disorder exhibited by some individuals when visiting or going on vacation to Paris, as a result of extreme shock derived from their discovery that Paris is not what they had expected it to be. The reality doesn't match the fantasy they'd created. The condition is commonly viewed as a severe form of culture shock, but it is much more than that. The difference between what a tourist expects to find in Paris and what they actually experience can be so jarring that it sometimes causes such symptoms as anxiety, delusions, and feelings of prejudice.

Of course, this doesn't just happen when we travel; it's a phenomenon that affects people in their everyday lives, too. In fact, unmet expectations seem to be one of the greatest factors contributing to our lack of joy. You may have a fantasy of moving abroad, or starting your own company, or starting a family, or having the "perfect" body, but when you actually reach that goal, you wonder why it feels so different from what you thought. And when your expectations don't match up with your experience, you can fall into a state of anxiety, stress, or self-blame.

Having a negative reaction when we are experiencing something we expect to be good sets us on a path toward looking for relief in the next big thing, and when we're disappointed again, we are off on a hamster wheel, always running to something new but never getting anywhere.

In theory, the answer would appear to be to have no expectations, but that's easier said than done. The focus on dreaming of a better tomorrow isn't just our own belief, it's our parents', our ancestors', our teachers', our society's, so it's been ingrained in us to dream and hope those dreams are fulfilled.

It becomes even more problematic when our dreams are imposed upon us. So many of us feel pressure from various sources to want to be and do and have certain things. Sometimes it's difficult to figure out whose dreams we are chasing.

I am a single woman in my late thirties and the only cousin on my mom's side who isn't married and doesn't have at least one child. The pressure I used to feel to get married and have kids was tremendous. My grandma would often say to me, "Time is ticking; if you want to have kids you better hurry up!"

Even my mom would make comments now and again. It was hard to for me to feel comfortable with who and where I was.

The pressure we get from loved ones and society can be so intense it can also make us feel like we are doing life wrong. Sometimes these demands aren't the same expectations you have for yourself. I wanted to be free to travel the world, to write, speak, and coach from anywhere, so I stayed mortgage-less and childless and significant-other-less for a few years by choice. (Not to say you can't do what you want with a family or home; it's all about priorities.)

So many of us put expectations on others, situations, things, and ourselves. We hope they will bring us joy. This is also why others put expectations on you. Mothers who keep pressing you to have a baby, fathers who keep asking about when you will get your promotion, pushing the issue because they think what they are hoping for you will bring you joy because it will bring them happiness. My mom wanted so much to be a grandmother, and for years her comments about wishing I wanted to have a child rather than travel made me feel like something was wrong with me. That is, until I realized she was putting her joy onto me. There's nothing wrong with her expressing what she wants, but sometimes we pressure others without even realizing it. Check in with yourself and think about your loved ones and your circle of friends. Are you feeling pressure to do something you don't really want to do because of their expectations of joy? When you recognize whose expectations are pushing you, you can then break free of them. Everyone is different. There is no one thing to make every single person happy. Let your own joy guide you. But, in order to release the pressure and expectations from others, we have to get clear about our own needs and truest desires. You have your own set of values, needs, and desires.

Think about the expectations others put on you, but also the ones you put on yourself. Recognize that expectations can never be as fulfilling as we hope, because joy is something that doesn't come from the outside, it comes from within. We don't find it. We allow it.

When you know and give yourself what you truly need, you no longer need the approval or validation from others.

Once I realized this, my entire experience transformed. I arrived in cities like Barcelona, Spain, and Zagreb, Croatia, with a grin on my face. Locals wondered why I was so happy. It was because I released all expectations and allowed myself to be comfortable with where I was instead of focusing on the next destination. I stopped needing things outside of myself to bring me joy and let my joy come from within.

That was the first massive shift for me. Instead of feeling like I couldn't be happy with where I was, I learned how to be happy with *who* I was, and that made all the difference. I used to think I didn't belong or fit anywhere, but when I released my expectations, I saw that I fit everywhere because I was finally comfortable with myself. How did I truly arrive to a place where I no longer needed the next best thing to make me happy? I uncovered what it is I truly needed.

Traveling the world full-time gave me a great insight into human nature and what it means to be alive. I discovered that no matter where in the world, people—regardless of cultural or religious background—all want the same thing. Of course, we all want safety, security, and love. In addition, we all want to be understood for who we really are and to express our true self, and this means we all, at the core of our being, crave belonging.

In the book, *The Power of Meaning* by University of Pennsylvania professor Emily Smith, evidence is shown that people who rate their lives with the most satisfaction are people with intense feelings of belonging and purpose. We want to feel like we are part of something bigger than ourselves; this gives us a sense of belonging.

A sense of belonging is a fundamental human need, just like the need for food and shelter. We can get this need met in many ways: through family, friends, church community, cultural activities, even uplifting social media. Some get a sense of belonging from deep connection with one or two people. Others feel connected to people in large groups or communities. Your joy could be eluding you because you're looking to see where you belong.

Many of us seem to be on a constant quest for belonging. We don't have a strong sense of connection and we struggle with feeling like we don't fit in anywhere. This is when loneliness occurs. While I was traveling, my sense of belonging was questioned; I didn't know where I fit. I was traveling solo, so I had more time for self-reflection. Most of my life, I never felt like I fit in. I always felt like I was in the outside looking in. This traced back to my childhood of not fitting in with the other kids, and often being ridiculed for doing things I naturally wanted to do.

But as an adult this pattern persisted. This happens to most of us: We have a traumatic or disturbing situation as a child, and we close off a part of ourselves as we grow into adults. We shy away from being who we really are because we are scared. We think things like, *It didn't work out for us last time, so why bother?* We don't want what happened then to happen to us again. This is a common defense mechanism. It's called emotional trauma. Emotional trauma creates mental blocks that prevent us from living our truest potential, and we can't move forward in life if we don't address it. Your true self knows that you are safe, because you are love. But our fears have us believe otherwise.

What are the patterns that have persisted from your own childhood? How are you blocking yourself from letting joy in because you are trying to protect yourself?

Joy Jaunt: Get Unstuck

In order to move forward and create the life we want, we have to identify the emotional barriers blocking us. Do this exercise in your joy journal for more clarity and direction.

1. Identify the pattern or behavior you would like to change (such as overeating, overspending, picking fights, procrastinating, etc.).

2. Identify how this behavior has helped you and kept you safe. (*Ex: I used to overeat because I wanted protection from a world I didn't trust or feel safe in. The extra padding on my body helped me feel protected from an unpredictable world.*)

3. Evaluate how this habit has harmed you and prevented you from feeling like your best self. (*I felt uncomfortable in my body and didn't love myself.*)

4. Create a new, more uplifting, and joyful pattern by identifying other ways to meet the same need.

(I can partake in activities such as nature walks, meditation, calling a friend, and cuddle sessions with my dog instead of overeating.)

5. Create an environment to support who you want to be and who you're becoming.

—————————————————————————

It wasn't until I started doing more research into the psychology of human behavior and writing this book that I noticed what patterns were hindering me. But further introspection led me to an even more important insight. If one of the most basic human needs is feeling connected and having a sense of belonging, and yet we're always struggling to find where we fit, perhaps the problem isn't that there is nowhere we fit, but that we consider ourselves unworthy of fitting anywhere. Perhaps the issue isn't outside of ourselves, but within. It seems for many of us, we don't feel a sense of connection with our own self.

Brené Brown wrote an article for *O, The Oprah Magazine* called "5 (Doable) Ways to Increase the Love in Your Life." In it she explains that 15 to 20 percent of folks are living with their whole hearts, and they were the people who deeply believed that they were *worthy* of love and belonging—regardless of the circumstances. Unfortunately, the majority of us aren't so confident in our worth. We think, *Okay, I'm worthy of love and belonging a little bit, but I'll be super worthy if I get promoted.* Or, *I'll be super worthy if I lose twenty pounds.* The people who were content in their life and felt satisfied with what was were the folks who believed that they were lovable and that they had a place in the world, and those beliefs translated into specific choices they made every day.

What I wondered was, how do the rest of us cultivate these same qualities? It's not like we can just decide to be worthy and say, "Hey, I belong because I'm worthy," after which—poof—this instantly comes true. But in the article, Brené Brown writes that our beliefs and how we see ourselves and the world affects our capacity to feel joy. Which means our beliefs and perceptions can actually be a contributing factor to our lack of connection to our self and others. The good news is that there are practical changes you can make in your life that can encourage new beliefs, which is exactly what I did to release my shame of feeling like I didn't belong and was worthless.

Here are seven ways to connect to your true self so you can feel a sense of belonging.

1. Let Go of Expectations

Our expectations will rob us of joy. When we expect things to be a certain way, we miss the awesome opportunities that could be happening instead. What expectation are you ready to release?

2. Go with the Way Things Are Going

When things don't go our way, we tend to get upset. But if we can go the way things are going, then we find harmony. I practiced being present and accepting what is, and saw that there is great freedom in the release. We can have an amazing time just enjoying the present and the unfolding of life. Can you stop trying to control your outcome and release expectations? Let things be what they are and go with the way they are going. You'll feel so much better.

3. Plan Less So You Can Live More

John Lennon said, "Life is what happens to you while you're busy making other plans." Whether we are traveling or in our own community at home, planning everything out can often stifle our creative expression. Life can't surprise us; there are no wow moments to be experienced when you have everything planned out. Instead of trying to control everything, relax a little and leave room for surprises.

We put so much pressure on ourselves to have everything figured out. While traveling, my itinerary was carefully planned down to the hour. About two weeks into my trip, I recognized how limiting that was. So I let go of the structure and dived deeper into each moment. It led to so many amazing experiences that never would have happened if I was sticking to a plan. This doesn't just apply to travel. It is about every area of your life. Where are you over-planning? We try to control our life because we feel out of control in certain areas. But when we let life take us where it wants to go and we trust the journey, we can experience so much more fulfillment and joy. The universe has a plan so much greater than your own.

4. Choose Passion and Purpose

The power of feeling connected to something larger than yourself is also about a sense of purpose. You have a purpose and it doesn't always look like one thing. So often we think we need to do one job or have one clear mission, but your life is a tapestry of experiences and options. Instead of focusing so much on purpose, just live more on purpose and let your passion lead you.

5. Play More

We live in a society in which people wear exhaustion as a badge, trying to one up each other with how busy they are. In fact, we don't know how to rest or play and we feel guilty when we take time to enjoy the simple things. When was the last time you did something just for fun? Although I had a website called Play with the World for years, I hardly ever played. I loved what I did so much, and my writing and coaching felt like play, but no matter how much I enjoyed it, it was work. It occurred to me that working all the time, no matter how much I love it, couldn't be good. I was shutting myself off from the rest of my life. All work and no play will keep us trapped in a bubble, with the rest of the world passing us by. Furthermore, we are layered beings, and we can't get fulfillment from just one place. Wanting to find all my joy in my work is unbalanced, so I set out to do more playful things, take part in activities that I love, and by bringing play into my life I expanded my world.

What do you love to do? Do more of it!

―――――――

Joy Jaunt: Play with the World

Sit down and make a list of non-work-related things that you love to do, things that make you lose track of time. You can invite loved ones to do the same and share your lists with one another. After you identify things you enjoy, you can create playdates with one another that will also help you feel more connected and give you a sense of belonging.

6. Come Together

One way to work on increasing your sense of belonging is to look for ways you are similar with others instead of focusing on ways you are different. When we can accept others for who they are instead of who we think they need to be, we can feel freedom within.

There is a lot of separation and exclusion in the world right now. This pushing apart only makes us feel a deeper longing for connection. You can choose to come together by opening yourself up to be more accepting of and kind to others. No matter what their background, beliefs, or point of view is, aim to value everyone's perspective.

A sense of belonging to a community improves our motivation, mental state, and health. You will soon see that you are not alone and there is comfort in knowing you are part of something greater than yourself.

7. Practice Self-Love

Another way to feel like you belong is to practice self-love. When we take care of ourselves and love ourselves, we feel more whole and complete. Therefore, it is a lot easier to connect with others and accept where we are in life. Emily Smith cites in her book, *The Power of Meaning*, that self-indulgence is critical to enjoying a life of the highest quality. However, living a life solely for yourself will become exhausting and shallow. You will want more depth and connection. The people who end up having the highest quality of life are those who have both self-indulgence and some sort of purpose in their day. To feel more joy in your life, schedule time for one or two activities that feel purposeful, and don't be afraid to have more fun. Making fun a focus will drastically improve your overall well-being.

> *Joy doesn't come from what you do, but in being who you are, as you are.*

When you adopt this perspective, you will no longer feel like you don't belong, nor will you feel insignificant, because you will feel so connected to yourself. Things outside of ourselves can induce joy, things like puppies, children, more abundance, romantic love, or even traveling to exotic locations. But if we aren't connected to our true self, the joy they bring will be fleeting. People can have riches beyond compare and still not have pure joy. This is why many celebrities who have money and fame report being extremely depressed and unhappy. As Jim Carrey, the comedian and actor, said, "I think everybody should get rich and famous and do everything they ever dreamed of so they can see that it's not the answer." Pure joy must come from deep inside us. It comes with knowing who you are and honoring your true self and not giving away your power. But this requires practice. It needs to be relearned, worked on, and nurtured from the inside out. And that is the journey you are diving deeper into. It is the most extraordinary journey of your life, for the rewards are immense.

Radical Recap

JOY BUSTER (expectations): Wanting things to be different than they are. Not accepting what is.

AWESOME OPPORTUNITY: Find your sense of belonging and connection by trusting and being yourself.

MANTRA: "My joy is not outside of myself. I cultivate it within."

When Helping Hurts

——

LET GO OF OVER-GIVING

Discomfort is a wise teacher.

—CAROLINE MYSS

ONE OF THE MOST OVERLOOKED ways we become disconnected from our joy is by overextending ourselves. You're probably a lot like me: You have a big heart, and you care deeply about those around you. You want to help and support those you love. Giving of your time, money, and energy is a beautiful thing, but sometimes we over-give at the expense of ourselves.

For many years, as I built my coaching practice, I would bend over backward to show up for clients, often answering emails late into the evening, taking emergency calls at all odd hours (that often weren't emergencies after all), and lowering prices to accommodate all people. I wanted so much to be of service and help others that I didn't even realize it was hurting my own health. Over time, I noticed that

I was isolating myself and overeating. I had gained a lot of weight and had chronic headaches and digestive issues. I kept wondering what was wrong with me. Why was it so hard to lose weight? Why was my stomach always in a knot? And why did I have random back and body aches? Plus, whenever I would go on vacation, I would get sick. For years this was my normal... until one day, I talked to my friend Suzi Southworth, an intuitive counselor, who said I was experiencing "compassion fatigue." I immediately went online to research this concept and found that this was exactly what I was suffering with.

When we experience overwhelming volumes of information—especially information that holds an emotional charge—our bodies, minds, and spirit adapt to help us cope. At times, the way we cope may help in the moment but may have negative long-term results. With the work that I was doing as a coach and a retreat leader, I was holding on to the life stresses of the people I wanted to help, without even realizing it. By being exposed to their situations, I was taking them on as my own.

Mothers, caregivers, coaches, wellness leaders, authors, therapists, teachers—basically anyone who cares for others and lends a listening ear to help support people—could be experiencing compassion fatigue. Compassion fatigue is a form of burnout that manifests itself as physical, emotional, and spiritual exhaustion. It is basically the emotional residue or strain of exposure to people who are suffering or have experienced stressful events. Even though your life may be fine, as you help others—even by just being a friend and constant companion—you could be taking on their pain as a subconscious way to help.

Common signs of compassion fatigue:

- Constant tiredness, even after resting
- Physical body tension
- Headaches, back pain, and wrist pain
- Falling sick when you have time to rest, such as on a vacation
- Feeling disconnected from your emotions and/or your body
- Feeling like no matter how much you give, it will never be enough
- Feeling helpless or hopeless about the future
- Increased levels of anger, irritability, resentment, or cynicism
- Using behaviors to escape, such as eating, taking alcohol/drugs, watching TV, or shopping
- No separation of personal and professional time
- Lacking a personal life outside of work

If a life-distressing event is affecting others in your life, you could be feeling the effects and trying to take on their pain, as to lessen the impact on them. I see this in people who are caring for sick family members, wives who are emotional rocks for husbands going through trauma, and parents who have children who constantly get into trouble and need to be bailed out. You want so much to help, because of your big beautiful heart, but the emotional, physical, even spiritual cost is draining you.

We need to have coping mechanisms to be able to navigate the emotional wounds we all take on and carry around. And the good news is there are ways to fix this situation. But we first have to understand how much it is affecting us.

After talking some more with Suzi, I realized that not only was I emotionally taking on all of the pain to try to lessen it for those around me, I didn't have any personal boundaries. I wasn't setting any limits on what I would give others. I was in constant giving-mode, which may sound wonderful and generous, but I was depleting myself. It's no wonder I was physically exhausted and ill. Being compassionate is a beautiful way to connect and feed our soul, but we must be compassionate to ourselves first.

I cared so much for others and wanted to make sure they were all okay, but at that point in my life, I never stopped to ask myself if I was okay. I didn't allow myself to feel my feelings; they just got bottled up and pushed aside. The shift for me was when I started to put myself first and practice self-care activities. One of my favorite activities became automatic writing. Every morning I would spend five to ten minutes journaling and allowing my inner guide to direct the free write. In one of my morning meditations, I asked a question: How can I be of the highest service to my audience and clients? You see, up until that point, I never felt like what I was doing was enough. I always felt like I needed to be doing more, reaching more, trying to help humanity in the biggest way possible. But that morning, when I did my free writing, I looked down at my paper and saw the words, "To serve others, we must first serve ourselves, take care of you."

I was shocked. I thought I *was* taking care of myself. In fact, I had just written an entire book about self-love, and the foundation in self-care. I thought to myself: *I work out daily, I drink a lot of water, and I am compassionate to myself. I get eight-plus hours of sleep each night, take daily nature walks, Epson salt baths and meditate. I mean, come on, what am I missing?* Why in the world was my direction to take care of myself when I was already doing so much? But when I dug a little deeper and decided to be more honest with myself, I saw that my body was still extremely overweight, I still had headaches, and I had no work–life balance. I still worked until midnight, I hadn't dated in five years, and I took vacations to "write and coach" but never really put my computer away. There was no boundary between what I did for a living and me. I always believed that since I loved what I do so much and it is my passion, that my work was feeding me and bringing me joy. But perhaps I was still missing the point.

My joy was just outside my reach because I was still escaping parts of my life. I was still overeating, watching mindless TV, and isolating myself. This was the side effect of caring so much about others that I forgot about myself. I knew I needed to make some changes. I revised my coaching schedule to allow more time for me. This led to taking an entire month off from working with clients and going on a real vacation. I went to a healing center in Costa Rica and practiced radical self-care. While in meditation, my inner voice said:

"Your life is about you. Stop making it about everyone else. To support others, you must first support you."

This sounds simple and we've heard this before. The problem is, I thought I was supporting myself. But upon a more honest look, I was just coping and trying to manage the discomfort. It wasn't until I let my discomfort be my teacher that I transformed my life. Today, I have a strong connection and powerful relationship with my body and my soul and I take care of me first. I have boundaries and do my work 110 percent when I'm working, but make myself a priority when I'm not. This has impacted my professional life in a powerful way. I can now be of the highest service to my clients because I feel vibrant and cared for myself.

Many of us have it reversed. We show up for others because we want so much to help but we completely forget about ourselves. No one tells you how to show up for you. There is no curriculum on how to be there for yourself. But we must be there for ourselves first. Even Mother Teresa understood compassion fatigue. She wrote in her plan to her superiors that it was *mandatory* for her nuns to take an entire year off from their duties every four to five years to allow them to heal from the effects of their caregiving work. As a caregiver, lover, helper, healer, light worker, and big-hearted person, whether it is your profession or you are simply giving to your family and friends, it is paramount we show up for ourselves first. It's not from a place of self-serving or ego driven, but a place of compassion, love, and genuine care. The only way to feel balanced, connected to our true self, and aligned with joy is to show up for you daily. And it isn't just eating healthy and working out. Self-care is so much deeper; it is about strengthening your relationship by nurturing you. Being in constant communication with your body and true self is optimal self-care.

Joy Jaunt: Overcome Over-giving

If you find yourself over-giving and are experiencing compassion fatigue, these methods can help.

1. Set Boundaries

As Shonda Rhimes says in her book *Year of Yes*, "No is a complete sentence." Learning how to say no and set personal boundaries can help you reclaim your power and feel more balanced.

2. Step Up Your Self-Care Routine

Self-care is not just drinking green juice and doing yoga daily. It can be your mental self-care routine, your physical, emotional, and spiritual routine, too. Look at each bucket of your life and create a self-care routine to help support the emotional, mental, physical, and spiritual sides of you.

3. Connect with Your Inner Child

We all have hidden sources of energy and healing power, things we loved to do as a kid such as draw, paint, or play in nature. Do more of this as an adult and let yourself be in the beauty of the moment.

4. Pause in Your Pleasure

Nurture yourself by putting activities in your schedule that are sources of pleasure, joy, and diversion. Allow yourself to take mini-escapes. These relieve the intensity of your life and allow you to be present with your own true self. Focus on purpose and passion. When you identify the things that fuel you, the things that you have true passion for, your fatigue can disappear.

5. Find Ways to Acknowledge Your Own Unhealed Loss and Grief

As a big-hearted person, you may be helping others as a subconscious way to cope with your own loss and grief. Let yourself grieve and give yourself permission to feel all the feelings associated with loss. If you need to see a professional—a life coach or therapist—please seek this support as it can help heal the pain.

6. Practice Self-Compassion

To prevent or recover from compassion fatigue, take time for self-reflection, identify what's important, and live in a way that reflects it. Be kind to yourself with kind words and nurturing activities.

7. Automatic Write

Sit down with your journal and ask a question, such as, What do I need right now? Or, What is the best way to care for myself? And let yourself write. Don't edit, just let it flow. Do this for five to ten minutes a day to really establish a strong relationship with yourself and intuition.

Radical Recap

JOY BUSTER: Over-giving.

THE FIX: Set boundaries.

MANTRA: "When I show up for myself, I can better support others."

Disconnected Detours

—

LET GO OF THINKING YOU DON'T MATTER OR FIT IN

> *To be truly happy, you need a clear sense of direction. You need a commitment to something bigger and more important than yourself. You need to feel that your life stands for something, that you are somehow making a valuable contribution to your world.*
>
> —BRIAN TRACY

THE FIRST DAY I WAS in Havana, Cuba, I pulled out my camera in a park next to the room I was renting, and I started taking pictures of the buildings. The architecture was gorgeous—a mix of neoclassicism, art deco, and colonial, so bold, classic, and fresh with the bursts of bright color. The colors ranged from electric blue and pastel pink to lime green. There I was soaking in the beauty, and a Cuban woman in her mid-seventies came near and started talking to me aggressively in Spanish. I didn't understand much of what she said, but I did hear "*No importante*" as she spun her pointer finger around, then pointed it at my camera. I smiled shyly and said, "*Gracias*," as to say thank you for sharing your opinion, and she nodded proudly and scurried off. What I gathered from our mini-exchange was she was politely telling me that this park is not important and I should not take photos of things that do not matter. As she walked away, I thought about the gravity of her message. It's not what she said that stayed with me, but how she said it. She was so passionate in her argument against photos in the park, which reminded me that everything is subject to perception and interpretation. I thought it was important, but another person can have a totally different point of view. There is a power that comes from having an opinion, and standing for something, anything, even if it is the opposite of others.

I used to be afraid of standing up, sharing my beliefs or speaking my point of view out loud with others. I actually didn't have a strong opinion about anything. I never wanted to rock the boat or cause any ripples. This approach to life left me lifeless and numb. I never had any substantive or real, meaningful conversations. There was no passion, no pulse. What the woman in the park reminded me of is how important it is to be passionate about something, anything, even if it's simply not taking photos in a park. What I am getting at here is, we have to stand for something if we want to be fulfilled in our life. When we are stuck, we don't usually give ourselves permission to have opinions. We hide our thoughts from others because we don't want to show people the real us, but so often we do this because we don't know who the real us even is. We've been conditioned to go along with the crowd, society, our family, culture, and the mainstream so anything that is different is foreign to us. Yet inside, we silently hurt, because we know on a soul level, even if we are still unconsciously aware, that we do have a point of view and our perspectives do matter.

Standing for something is about you being more honest with yourself about what you truly care about. I'm not talking about being argumentative or defensive about your beliefs, but simply speaking your truth. The goal of being passionate about things and standing for something is not necessary to get others to believe the same as you or come support you. Your passion is yours. It is for you and only you, it brings you joy and that is the point. We all know those people who get argumentative about their beliefs, and they think you are wrong if you don't support what they care about. This is not what I mean when I say stand for something, because when we are defensive about our beliefs, this is actually a fear-based reaction. When we need others to believe what we believe, it is because there is a part of us that does not feel strong enough in our own convictions. The balance we truly seek, and ultimate goal, is to be able to stand in our truth by owning unapologetically what we care about.

"The fear of being different forces me to be like everyone else."
—Meera Lee Patel

It is important to believe what you want and what makes sense for you, and be comfortable enough in your own beliefs that you can let others believe what they wish. This can feel like a challenge because we are so used to going through the motions of life and trying not to rock the boat or cause more drama. We hide ourselves from others because we are terrified of not being understood or liked. Most often we don't yet understand or like ourselves. Part of why we feel off is because we are hiding our true selves. The moment you begin to speak from your heart and say what you need and want to say, your life feels better. When you start to ask yourself, "What do I care about? What do I stand for?" you start to believe more in yourself. And by believing in yourself, you are more present and connected to yourself and others.

Today I am unapologetic about my lifestyle, my needs, my beliefs, and my dreams. I am so connected to my belief system that it gives me power and focus to move forward. That's what happens when we believe in things that make us feel good. We show up more fully in our own life because we are connected to our true self.

We all get something specific from our belief systems; some need security, purpose, community, while others need structure, reward, or power. The beliefs don't define us, and they don't make others wrong if they are different from ours. We have to trust that everyone gets what they need from their own belief system. For example, I have a good friend who used to be an atheist. She didn't believe in God. Over the past few years she's been through some traumatic events and is now going through a divorce. She has recently changed her beliefs, has turned to God, and this is helping her through the traumatic time. We get what we need when we need it, and our beliefs help us through all phases of our life.

In the book *A Course in Miracles*, Helen Schucman, Ph.D., a clinical and research psychologist asks, "Would you rather be right or happy?" I interpret this to mean that being right is not as fulfilling as being happy.

We need to remember that our beliefs don't make us right; we believe them because they make us happy.

Focus on beliefs that work for you, but don't be afraid to change. As you grow, your beliefs will, too. In order to move out of your frustration, establish a belief system and identify with ideals and values that are important to you, for this act of caring about something is an act of self-love. You start to identify with who you are in the world, and this guides you forward.

Align yourself with beliefs that mean something to you. I've witnessed coaching clients and friends go through this process and decide they want to change religions, locations, change relationships, or careers. You might not have all the clarity on how at this point, and that's okay. For now, you are planting the seeds to open up into more of your true self so you can be happier in your life. The point is, we can admit what we want most at any age and stage of our life. The goal is to honor the inner voice that is speaking to you. The one that says, "Hey this is important to you. Go for this." The inner voice that says, "I agree with this. I don't like that. I am going to speak up on this topic. I will stand for this." Being passionate about things shows that you care. It means you are participating in life.

No one can tell you what is important to you. This is something you discover for yourself. Each one of us is different, so what brings one person joy might not elicit the same response in another, but that's the point. To be on this planet with lots of different perspectives and values is totally okay. If we all believed, thought and wanted the same things, life would be incredibly boring.

Joy Jaunt: Stand for Something

Sometimes we can't access our joy because we are afraid to speak up. We get comfortable not rocking the boat, but this leads to uncomfortable results.

Moving forward in life means you believe in something that makes you feel good. To identify what you truly stand for, ask yourself key questions:

- Where are you afraid to speak up?
- What part of your life are you settling in and not willing to rock the foundation?
- Where are you sacrificing yourself to keep others happy?
- What steps can you take to share your truth?
- How can you get more involved with your passion?

The contrast of life is what gives us clarity.

If you are stuck in what you don't want, then see this as an opportunity to gain a deeper understanding of what you do want.

If you feel stuck in any area of your life, chances are it's because you are hiding a piece of you that wants to be expressed.

A fast way to overcome feeling stuck and off track is to stand up for something that you believe in. I am not necessarily talking about starting a movement, joining a cause, or overhauling your life to stand up for something that is important to you (although if you feel moved to do that, by all means rock on, soul sister or mister). What I am simply sharing is an opportunity for you to feel more connected to your own life by connecting to what is important to you. It has to start with passion and aligning with your own joy.

Right after my doctor diagnosed me with depression, I knew I wanted more for myself and life. I was passionate about animals and helping the planet, so I started volunteering my time at local animal shelters. This inspired me to eventually get my own dog, and each step helped pull me out of depression. I also loved art and used to paint, so I got back into painting for a couple years, and the proceeds earned went directly to the World Wild Life Foundation, a nonprofit that protects endangered animals. Today I donate a percentage of the profits from my meditation albums to animal rescues, like Golden Bond. The idea is to align with your values, because when you live your values you feel more connected to your life. Things become more meaningful and enjoyable. You have a sense of purpose. Identify what you care about. Then once you identify this, take action to create the lifestyle that aligns with these values.

Get clear about what is important to you and be okay with changing your beliefs. Sometimes *what* we think and believe is the reason we are stuck still. Many times our beliefs are really fears trying to keep us safe but actually stifling our growth. What beliefs are holding you back? Do you feel like you can't make money doing what you love? Do you feel like going after what you want is selfish? Do you feel like you don't deserve to be happy? Do you feel like your higher power has abandoned you? These are common beliefs I hear from my life coaching clients, and ones I held, too. Once I realized they were just fears, I stopped believing them and changed my thoughts to focus on the positive ones.

The beliefs we cling to that are limiting us are the disconnected detours. They keep us from moving forward in our life. Detours don't always help us. They are a route we take that leads us in a different direction, and they are disconnected when we are focusing on beliefs that hinder us. Oftentimes detours make it take longer for us to get to where we want to go. When we hold on to our limiting beliefs, we are inevitably on a path that will take us much longer to arrive at fulfillment. In order to move forward and get back to your true self, connect with beliefs that feel uplifting and joyful. You know you have a limiting belief when it makes you feel constricted and depressed, sad, or anxious. Beliefs such as, *I will never be happy* or *I'll never figure it out* or *Something is wrong with me* are all thoughts that make you feel less than. That's how you know they are limiting. Let go of these beliefs and focus on more expansive, joyful ones like, *All is well* or *Nothing is wrong with me. I am learning and growing and I trust the process.* And *The universe is supporting me.*

Identify your beliefs, the thought patterns you've been stuck in, and see which ones can shift. Once you do this, everything can change in your life.

Radical Recap

JOY BUSTER: Fear of not fitting in, or thinking we don't matter.

THE FIX: Use your voice, share your opinions, show more of the true you.

MANTRA: "I focus on feeling good and align with beliefs that support my well-being."

The Good Fear

LET GO OF LETTING FEAR CONTROL YOU

*Boredom, anger, sadness, or fear are not "yours,"
not personal. They are conditions of the human
mind. They come and go. Nothing that comes
and goes is you.*

—ECKHART TOLLE

ABOUT A WEEK BEFORE I left for my trip around the world, I woke up one morning with a huge pain in my chest. I felt short of breath and my thoughts were very fuzzy and confused. My inner voice was one of fear and it was loud. It said:

"Who do you think you are? Traveling for a year is so
extreme. You are so stupid and silly."

"You're crazy."

"What are you trying to prove?"

"This is the dumbest thing you've ever done."

"It's not going to work out."

"It's not too late to back out."

This voice was so incredibly uncomfortable that my daily actions were actually hindered. Fear can do that. It can manipulate us. It will cause us physical discomfort and try to derail our life plan. This type of fear keeps us numb and forces us to ignore our true self.

Luckily, even though I hadn't started traveling, I was already on my Joy Seeker Journey. In the past, when my fear voice was loud, my inner faith muscles would not have been strong enough to quiet it. I would have quietly slipped back into a miserable job and stayed in a relationship that didn't make me feel good. I would have sacrificed who I really wanted to be because fear was winning. I would have tried to convince myself it wasn't that bad. Meanwhile my soul would have been suffocating. When fear takes over, most of us will be so uncomfortable with this emotional pain that we will retreat. We go back on our word, we give up, we cancel our plans. We stay in the situation we know we want to leave. Basically, we let fear win and stay stuck in a static routine and a joyless life.

I was far enough along in my own journey to know that fear can be part of our life at any stage and will always pop up when we are approaching something new. And not all fear is negative. Good fear doesn't want to stop you. It simply wants to protect you, and as long as it knows you are safe, then you can coexist with your fear.

This dream, to travel the world, was a big deal. I was playing full out, so my fear was louder than ever. Before leaving, I had thoughts of canceling my trip, throwing in the towel, but I knew well enough that if I just felt the fear and sat with it, it would subside. And it did. About forty-eight hours later, my excitement returned and I was ready to follow through on my goal. Here's what we need to know about our fears: They aren't all bad and they aren't something that needs to stop us. Fear is present when we are disconnected from our truth, when we disengage with our inner light. Fear, as you may have heard before, represents False Evidence Appearing Real. My fear tried to convince me that I wasn't worthy of living my dreams and my trip would be a big flop, but this was a false reality. Don't believe your fear.

We all have fear—fear of failing, fear of the unknown, fear that we are off track, fear of what others will think. But all of this is just part of being alive. Instead of fighting or fearing our fear, we can befriend it.

To be human is to feel fear. Don't run from it or let it take over and lead you. When we don't understand our fear, we often find ways to distract ourselves to help us handle the pain. I don't want to be a person who escapes life; I want to feel it and be fully in it. When you give yourself permission to dive fully into your life, the fear naturally goes away, because you are living your truth. I saw that my fear wasn't as bad as I thought because most of our fear is in our mind, and I learned that when fear is present it means that we're growing.

Fear can be a compass. It shows up to help you address where you've been playing it safe.

⌒

Feel your fear, let it work through you and know that you do not have to run away from it or overcome it. When we recognize that we can indeed exist with our fear and accept ourselves, lovingly, alongside our fear, our world will transform. Most of us are troubled by fear because we think

Joy Jaunt:

What am I most afraid of ?

FEAR OF THE
UNKNOWN

FEAR OF FAILURE

FEAR OF
LONELINESS

*Your
Inner
world*

FEAR OF
REJECTION

FEAR OF
LOSS

FEAR OF LOSING
MY FREEDOM

FEAR OF
BEING UNLOVED

FEAR OF NOT BEING
ACCEPTED
OR GOOD ENOUGH

on some level we aren't supposed to have it. But fear is meant to guide us. Instead of running from your fear, embrace it, and see it as directing you onto a path to freedom. Let the fear crack you open to reveal your truth. But don't stay in the fear. As soon as you see it, the moment you feel it, take action to move through it. You do this by inviting love and light in. Love is your truth. You don't have to believe the fear or allow it to consume you; you can simply love it for trying so hard to protect you. When you let your light shine brighter than your fear, you will be unstoppable and you will feel an inner peace you never thought possible.

Radical Recap

JOY BUSTER: Letting fear manipulate and control you. Allowing it to run the show.

AWESOME OPPORTUNITY: Love your fear. Instead of pushing it away, see it as an indicator of what you care most about.

MANTRA: "My fear is only an illusion. I detach from negative thoughts and habits and turn my attention to faith and love."

From Frozen to Freedom

LET GO OF HIDING YOUR TRUE SELF

*Fear is a natural reaction to moving closer to
the truth.*

—Pema Chodron

W HEN I WAS WORKING IN advertising and stuck in my depression, I would look at other people, like professional performers and musicians, and watch them perform. They represent people who are passionate about what they do for a living, and are using their skills and natural talent with great ease and joy. I'd be in awe of how in the moment they were and how effortless their joy seemed. It was obvious from their performances they were doing what they loved. You know when people are living their passion because they are so incredibly in the moment, and so joyful about the experience. They seem to express themselves with great ease and grace. This is passion in action. I wanted so much what they had, the connection to my life purpose. They had found their reason for being. I would think, They get to do what they love every day. It doesn't even feel like a job.

I made it a focus for my own life to find my passion and true purpose. I wanted to be as joyful and present as the people I admired who were doing what they loved. That is when I recognized my love of travel and writing. There was a freedom that took over when I wrote. I started writing for magazines and the local newspaper, and when I wrote my first book, *Find Your Happy*, I felt a freedom I had never known before. The thrill of being able to work from anywhere and express myself fully is my ultimate joy. You see, that is what joy is: freedom. Freedom to be who you really are, as you are, doing what you love. The more we commit to our joy, the easier our entire life will be. I focused on creating a life that encouraged me to do more of what I love, and today, after almost eight years of building my own business, I am writing this book from all over the world. Maybe you just read "eight years" and thought: *I don't have that kind of time to build my dream life. It will take too much time, money, and energy, and besides I don't know if it will work out.* Or did you think: *Wow, think of where I can be in eight years if I start today?* Two very different mind-sets that will predict your outcome.

Ask yourself, What is not going for the life you want costing you? Imagine where you will be in three, five, ten years if you don't intentionally create and aim for it. Where will you be if you continue to ignore your inner guide? Being miserable, depressed, anxious, and stuck is no way to live your life. But taking steps each day to add more joy into your life and following the inspiration from your heart will help tremendously by giving you an outlet of self-expression. In order to feel more peace, you need to do more of what you love and soon any anxiety you feel will be replaced with wonder.

Each step we take builds upon the next. And the past eight years have been incredibly important for building a solid foundation for me to be able to live my own potential and travel the world full-time—writing, coaching, and speaking my way around the globe, financially worry-free. Don't stress over how long it takes, because when you are doing what you love, time expands. So often we want to be further along than we are, and this prevents us from enjoying the present.

Whatever your dream is, get clear within yourself about what you want. And if you don't know what you want, a great starting point is to identify what you don't want. When I first left my job in advertising, I didn't know what I wanted but I knew what I was doing didn't feel good. I knew I wanted to live with more purpose and passion. I was very clear that I didn't want a corporate job and I wanted to be my own boss, and with each step I took away from what I didn't like, my life revealed more clarity.

A profound tool that helped me is the ideal life list. I asked myself: "If money, time, effort, and all things aside didn't matter and I knew I would succeed, what kind of life would I want?" Ask yourself this same thing. I wrote down things like being a bestselling author, leading retreats around the world, being a well-sought-after writer and wellness thought leader, having a blog that reached hundreds of thousands of people all over the world, speaking on stages across the globe and inspiring audiences to get in touch with their heart. When I wrote this list I was living in my parents' basement, on unemployment, and with no published work or any connections or real understanding of the industry. But today everything I listed is my reality, with the added bonus of being able to work from anywhere and travel the globe freely. Create your list, make that ideal life vision, and go for it. You need to create a blueprint for the life you want to build. Instead of repeating the refrain, "I don't know what I want," simply say, "I am open to learning more about myself."

Joy Jaunt: Create Your Ideal Life

If time, money, energy, resources, and other people weren't an issue, what would you want to do with your day?

How would you spend your life?

If you knew you could not fail, what would you do?

Trust this vision. This is who you really are and who you want to be. So get out your pen and paper and make your list. Don't be afraid to ask yourself, "What does my ideal life feel like?"

Radical Recap

JOY BUSTER: Not knowing what you want and avoiding passion and purpose.

AWESOME OPPORTUNITY: Get clear about your passion and what you love and focus on it daily.

MANTRA: "I deserve to live the life I know I am made for."

Release the Hostage Desires

LET GO OF THINKING IT NEEDS TO BE PERFECT

Perfection itself is imperfection.
—Vladimir Horowitz

MANY OF US PUT AN enormous amount of pressure on ourselves to have things look and seem a specific way; we want our lives to be *perfect*. Unfortunately, this quest for perfection keeps us from living our best life. We put our desires on hold and push them to the back burner because things don't *look* the way we think they should. Think of all we're missing out on! To truly connect to our joy, we have to bust through these barriers and release the pressure we put on ourselves.

Growing up, my parents enjoyed entertaining. They loved inviting people over and often had dinner parties. As a kid, I remember getting so excited when company arrived. The house was always full of laughter and good times. However, recently, I noticed a shift in my parents'—particularly my mother's—behavior. Over the past few years, my folks have been renovating their house. It's been a rather long process with work being done in stages and in different parts of the house. Last year, as my father's birthday approached, he suggested the family have a party at their home. But my mother went into combat mode and said, "The house is too dirty. There isn't enough time. We have too much work to do before people can come over. The dogs will need a bath," and so on. She talked my father out of having the party at the house because she didn't want company over to see the renovations until they were complete, until things were *perfect*. We ended up having a small get-together at a restaurant, and it felt rushed and not as fun as game night at home. Although we had a good time, it seemed my folks were disappointed as they realized they missed out on doing what they loved best—entertaining and having quality family time in a home they loved.

Can you relate? A lot of us want to connect with loved ones, but we look around our home and think there is too much work to do. We think our homes have to be perfect for guests, but this is again fear trying to keep us from feeling joy. What we really want is social time, community, connection, love, and support. Spending time with loved ones is one of the easiest ways to get these core needs met. Yet a part of our brain convinces us we need to change our environment before we can connect with others or be social. It is our fear of being judged and the rooted insecurity that we aren't good enough that fuels this behavior. Think about the parties you've gone to and social events you showed up for. Most of the time you are so happy to be there connecting with loved ones that you don't notice the things that are *off* or not in perfect order. Because it doesn't matter. The books in the corner, the chipped kitchen counter, the wall that needs new art, or the half-dead plant, it's all keeping us from connecting to each other and joy. When we do this, our desires are held hostage and we postpone our joy until our life *looks* and *feels* "perfect," but perfect is an illusion.

Sometimes we strive for perfection because we want to motivate ourselves. We think things like: *I will invite people over and have my dinner party after I paint the house* or *I will start dating when I lose ten pounds* or *I will ask for a promotion after I buy new clothes so that I can dress the part* or *I will write the book when I have more time.* We assume this line of thinking will get us to clean the house or follow through on the diet or get our wardrobe in order or actually carve out time in our schedule. But these are false promises hidden behind excuses. The true, real, authentic us knows that how things look is not as important as how things feel. Which means the real measure of happiness is you choosing joy, not putting it off.

One of the most memorable experiences of my travels was when I was invited into a Russian family's home for dinner in St. Petersburg. We didn't speak the same language, but we were able to connect over food. The family brought me into their home through a cultural exchange program. There was no translator, no real comprehension of language, yet we understood each other completely. We spoke with our eyes and hearts. We were thrilled to be together, connecting our cultures and differences, and shattering borders to unite in our humanity. The food brought us together, and as I looked around the traditional Russian home, I was overwhelmed with gratitude. I barely noticed that there were trinkets with dust built up on them, books shoved into all windowsills, and that the carpet was torn and ripping at the seams. I never once judged or thought twice about the appearance of the home, because I was fulfilling one of our deepest core needs, connection. One of the most impactful experiences of my life happened because pretenses of perfection were dropped.

Are you using excuses that prevent you from connecting with others? Instead of waiting till things look another way, go for your desires now. Break through the illusion of perfection and see that the real perfect moment is in our humanity and coming together. Give yourself permission to bring people into your life in a more natural authentic manner.

Radical Recap

AWESOME OPPORTUNITY: Wanting things to be perfect.
THE FIX: Come together and recognize life is happening now.
MANTRA: "My life is in perfect balance when I listen to my heart and follow through on my joy."

Look at Your Money, Honey

LET GO THINKING YOUR LIFE
WILL BE BETTER WHEN YOU
GET WHAT YOU WANT

*The fastest way to bring more wonderful exam-
ples of abundance into your personal experience
is to take constant notice of the wonderful things
that are already there.*

—ESTHER HICKS

I T WOULD BE DIFFICULT TO talk about living a fulfilled
life if we didn't look at our money habits, beliefs, and
concerns. So many people I know stress out over money. I
used to as well. The overload of negative emotions that many
of us experience in relation to our finances can prove an ob-
stacle when we want to experience unlimited joy. To
understand your stress triggers with money, an easy place to
start is to think about how you think about money. How
much time do you spend worrying about, thinking about, or
talking about it? This can be an indicator of your stress and
anxiety level. But the key thing to know is that if we want ful-

fillment, we need to focus on abundance and opportunity instead of lack and debt.

I've met so many people who are obsessed with their debt. They talk about it all the time and try to find ways to get out of it, but their focus on it keeps their debt from going anywhere. I've seen it happen to many people: They find a way to pay off their debt... that same debt they would always talk about and focus on, the one that if only they could pay this off their life would be better... they pay it off, using retirement funds, refinancing a home, or suddenly coming into a lot of money, and then within months of the "debt" being paid off they find themselves right back where they started with more bills and often even more debt than before. It's like diets: We go on them, lose weight, think our life will be better, then gain all the weight back and often even more. This happens because the debt or weight isn't the real problem. It's the inside of us that feels unworthy and undervalued and our outside world just reflects this. Healing needs to be an inside job. No matter how many breaks we get or opportunities to pay off the debt or lose the weight, we have to heal the inside in order to fix the outside.

The real key to healing from financial stress is to shift your focus from scarcity to prosperity. You attract what you focus on, and if you're always talking about lack, that's what you'll have. The only way to live in abundance is to focus on abundance. Shifting our focus from lack to abundance is a process, but it is one of the best ways to feel more joy in your life.

Don't be afraid to look at what you spend your money on. We can carve out a life that brings us joy by being passionate about the things we spend our time, money, and energy on. When you spend money, ask yourself, "Does this item I am purchasing or investing in bring me long-term joy?" Start to look at transactions as joy opportunities. When I was depressed and stuck in life, I feared money, I was in massive debt, and I was ignoring my financial responsibilities. But I recognized everything in our life is connected and how I spend my money and how I feel about money are connected to all other areas of my life, including my capacity to feel joy. I was focused so much on debt until I realized my focus on it was keeping me in it. So I changed the way I saw my financial situation by replacing the word *debt* with *investment*. The things I spent money on—putting myself through grad school, buying things for my place, travel, and so on—were investments, not problems. The word *investment* is uplifting and joyful because it shows that you are creating a life dedicated to growth. Plus this mind-set shift makes it more difficult to complain and worry about it. Instead of saying, "I have so much debt," you would want to celebrate, "I have so many investments," because investments are opportunities, advancement, and growth potential. Investment is joyful; debt is not. It is all about perspective and aligning yourself with something that feels good and full of possibilities, rather than restrictive and limiting.

Once I started to look at my money this way, things changed even more. I started to have a new *relationship* with money. Disrespecting it, refusing to be thankful for it, and always fearing I wouldn't have enough was a very unhealthy relationship. I used to hate money because I thought it was the source of my pain: *If only I had more money, I could do what I wanted.* I didn't realize it at the time, but this was just an excuse. When we're not clear about what we want, we blame things outside of ourselves. Money was my scapegoat. When I flipped the script and focused on what money could do *for* me, I developed an attitude of gratitude, respecting money, but not letting it have power over me.

MONEY IS AN IMPORTANT PART of our life; we can't deny that. We use it daily. And we should recognize that what we spend our money on is a reflection of our true self. Money is about value, and what you spend your money on shows what you value. Therefore, if you don't have a good relationship with money, you most likely don't have a strong relationship with yourself. If you fear it, hate it, ignore it, or spend past your means, it's because there is a part of you that feels unworthy. There is perhaps even a part of your life you are afraid to look at. Maybe there is a part of you that you are ignoring.

Sometimes our beliefs around money are fear manifesting itself into thought patterns that are just keeping us stuck. For many of us, we use spending as a way to cover up the fact that we aren't really fulfilled. We feel something is missing, so buying something new can help fix that pain. But it's fleeting and always leads to regret. Many of us spend well beyond our means on things that don't really bring us much joy, but we feel we need to buy: fancier cars, bigger homes, designer clothes, and handbags, and on and on. Although all of these may bring us temporary happiness, they don't necessarily have long-term impact. Don't get me wrong, I'm not saying you shouldn't want and buy nice things if you can afford them. But do they really bring you joy if shortly after you acquire them you are longing for the newest model, the latest edition, the new season's offerings? Too often we are buying things because we are told we should want them and acquiring them will bring us joy. But as I've said joy is an inside job. The deeper we go on this journey, the more you will realize that joy never comes from things, or even experiences. It is a feeling inside of us. Check in with yourself and see if you could be spending frivolously trying to find joy in outside sources. I did for many years and it never got me anywhere.

What are you spending your money on and why? Always ask, "Does it bring me joy?" A good way to know if you are wasting money on something that doesn't bring you joy is if you feel guilty after you buy it. When I travel, most of my spending is invested directly into experiences. As I visit places all around the world, I invest in museums, cultural events, specialty coffee and food experiences, tours, and events that will make an imprint on my mind and heart rather than a dent in my ego, inducing guilt because they are things that don't enrich my life.

You may be saying, "Okay, easy enough, but what about big bills, the mortgage, kids' college, the big life expenses that hang over us?" If your attitude when it comes to these things is, "I hate bills. They suck up all my money," then the experience of paying them will be pure torture. But everything is about perspective, so changing your focus to "I am thankful I have the money to pay for *this*" or "I am so happy I could make this investment," will be a game changer. Each time you pay a bill, no matter the size, and send it with love, be thankful for all the opportunity it provides in your life. This will reverse your "lack of" mentality and soon you will be so focused on abundance and joy that debt won't even be in your vocabulary. And with this approach, your debt will disappear.

> *When we shift our beliefs, we can radically change our results.*

Start to look at money as a friend. Much like your fear, it is in your life to support you. When you can look at money as a gift to you and you start to appreciate it, everything will change. I am able to travel the world full-time without worrying about money because I improved my own relationship with money by improving the relationship with myself. I did this by discovering my value and by finding self-love. I started to respect money because I respected myself. I thanked money. Even when I found a penny on the ground in a parking lot, I celebrated it. When I paid my bills, I would kiss the check and say thank you (a technique I learned from Louise Hay). This attitude of appreciation attracts more abundance into your life. Start to play in the joy of life and the abundant energy by thinking about money as a friend. Ask yourself, "What is my relationship to money? How can I be more thankful for the money I do have?"

What's really happening in this process of cleaning up your relationship with money is you are creating more peace in your life. Everything in your life is a relationship. You are in one with your money, your health, your career, your dreams. When you focus on having healthy relationships, you will remove anxiety from your life. From here on out, appreciate money like you would a dear old friend. Treat it kindly and spend it joyfully. Because it is in your life to support you.

Radical Recap

JOY BUSTER: Focusing on debt, lack, what you don't have.

AWESOME OPPORTUNITY: Invest in Joy. Be grateful for what you do have.

MANTRA: "I am supported and loved, I always have enough for I am enough."

Joy Seeker Journal Time

In your workbook or joy journal, take a moment to answer these questions before progressing to the next section.

- Where has fear been trying to stop me and prevent me from moving forward?
- What is my fear trying to tell me?
- When do I feel like my best self?
- When do I feel the most alive?

Let Go
OF THE
SEXY
Story

#JoySeeker

PART 2

THE RELEASING

How to Let Go of Thinking It Needs to Be Different

Feel to Heal

RELEASE THE BELIEFS
THAT NO LONGER SERVE YOU

*Humans have so many beliefs that contradict
their own desires, that they don't let themselves
realize or receive or witness the magic.*
—Abraham Hicks

E ALL EXPERIENCE SITUATIONS IN our life that can be painful, situations that make us uncomfortable. But often, time passes and we don't even remember them. This is our ego at work, suppressing these painful memories, trying to protect us from having to feel these emotions again. But the memories don't go away; we're just suppressing them in an effort to stay in control and have it together. And this defense mechanism causes a huge disconnect with ourselves and with others around us. So many of us are walking around as a fraction of who we really are. We live in a protective shell we've created to endure life's difficulties. The problem with this is, we not only stay at a distance from everyone, always judging, comparing, protecting ourselves and our hearts, but it also creates a massive hole inside of us. This hole is an emotional, invisible hole we try to fill with stuff, people, things, food, anything but what we truly need, which is to feel our feelings and let them be our teacher.

The key to transformation is in feeling our emotions—all of them, including those we have subconsciously repressed. We store emotions in the body—grief, fear, shame—they're all packed into parts of us, hidden away, they can even manifest as physical sensations, such as pain, and even illness. Oftentimes, these stored emotions feel like an emptiness, an insatiable deep pit within us, that we try to fill by overeating, overspending, overworking. But nothing seems to fill the emptiness, nothing ever seems enough, no matter what we do, *we feel as if we are* never enough. I know this all too well. For almost three full decades, this empty sensation of never feeling enough ruled my every action. I never felt full. *Ever.* I would eat past capacity, I would overwork—often sixteen to eighteen hours a day—I would exercise manically, I would go on shopping sprees, buying things I didn't even need. Everything was an attempt to try to fill up my emptiness inside. From where I am now, I can clearly see how I desperately tried to fill this emptiness with external solutions but nothing worked. It wasn't until I stopped looking outward and started leaning inward that I transformed my life.

It wasn't until I went to Costa Rica and participated in a weeklong wellness retreat, at Rythmia Life Advancement Center, that I saw how our unhealed past will play out in the present and dictate our future. While at the healing center, I participated in a shamanic journey and discovered the source of my never-ending emptiness. For almost thirty-five years of my life I felt unlovable, alone, and like I didn't belong or fit in. These beliefs felt very real. So real that they created my reality. I kept dating men who couldn't love me the way I needed. I would consistently find myself in social circles where people were making fun of me or talking behind my back and spreading rumors. I never felt like I fit in and I never felt good enough, and my experiences would always reinforce these beliefs. My life had a clear pattern: The belief that I was unworthy drove my behavior and dictated my experiences, and my experiences reinforced my belief. But in my shamanic journey I went back to the moment that birthed my feeling of unworthiness. I revisited my three-year-old self. I saw her crying out for help. She was scared, alone in her crib, trying so hard to get anyone's attention. I saw and felt how this little me felt in that moment. She was so terrified that she was alone in the world, and couldn't understand why she was asking, begging, reaching out for help, yet no one would come. In that exact moment, the belief that I am unlovable, I am alone, no one cares about me, was created. At age three my insecurities started. At age three, that little girl behind her crib bars felt emotions that were too painful to process, so she created a belief system to try to protect her and avoid ever having to feel this way again.

The shamanic journey took me back to my defining moment.

We all experience this moment. It is a moment that impacts us to such a degree that our worldview is developed. It usually happens between the ages of three and five, and is connected to a traumatic and emotionally intense

No one teaches us what to believe. We initially believe what we experience. Our beliefs create our reality.

⁓

situation. And it doesn't matter how intense the trauma. Pain is pain. It is in that moment that our worldview is developed to protect us from ever feeling that way again. It creates our belief system and how we see ourselves in the world. The problem is that the beliefs we create are all based on un-healed emotions and fear. We must return to that moment, confront the emotions, heal our pain, and find our truth.

We heal by releasing, not suppressing.

Feeling your emotions and revisiting your past pain points and traumas will help heal your destructive pattern forever. If we don't go into our past to heal, the patterns will persist throughout our entire lives. We will live our lives always feeling off, like something is missing, and we wonder why no matter what we try we can't lose weight, or we can't stop spending money or get out of debt, or keep a healthy relationship, or we can't be happy with where we are as we are. We wonder why, and it all circles back to an emotional trauma we've blocked ourselves from feeling. The key to transformation is to go into these experiences, dive into them, because the only way to is through.

It can be hard to think about or relive traumas from our past. In fact, many of us have actually blocked these parts of our lives out; we don't recall the memories because we think they are just too painful to process. But the only way to truly heal is to let ourselves feel. As soon as I recognized my life-long belief of not feeling good enough was tied to me being alone crying out for help at age three, I was able to disengage with this belief and rewrite my story. Recognize that every single human has a painful moment that defines them. The problem isn't painful experience; it is who we've become because of the beliefs that we created at the moment. In my shamanic journey, I saw firsthand the person I had become as a result of believing I am unlovable and unworthy. At that point in my life I had been single for almost six years, I was almost sixty pounds overweight, and I isolated myself and avoided social situations. At thirty-seven years old, I was overworked, alone, and scared of getting close to people. But once I saw clearly and honestly where my limiting beliefs came from and how they were damaging me, I could transform them. We have to be honest about who we have become as a result of believing these lies about ourselves. Sure I was happy, I felt self-love and I had a thriving business and writing career. But transformation requires radical honesty, and that means looking at all sides of ourselves, especially the parts we've been running from. As soon as I saw the root cause of my belief system, I could see that the overweight, insecure, lonely version of me was just a mask, a fake version of me created out of protection. It wasn't the real me. The real me is social, lovable, and full of energy and passion.

Everything comes back to the beliefs we have about ourselves. If there is a pattern or habit you have that you don't like, chances are beliefs about yourself are causing that pattern. When we reframe our beliefs, we transform our entire life.

Joy Jaunt: Eradicate Your Limiting Beliefs

If we want to transform our life, we have to look at our beliefs, and we do this by feeling the emotions and identifying where they started. It's important to get to the root cause of the limiting beliefs and see who you've become as a result. Ask yourself these key questions and take yourself on your own journey.*

1. How do you feel? (alone, sad, mad, frustrated, angry, etc.)
2. Do you usually feel this way in life? (Be honest with yourself. Hint: when you do this exercise right, the answer is almost always yes.)
3. When do you first recall feeling this way? (Go back to the pivotal moments in your life, most often between ages three and five, and recall all of the times you felt this way.) This is the defining moment.
4. What belief was created in this moment? How did you try to protect yourself?
5. Who have you become as a result of this false-based belief system?
6. Who am I really?

———————————

After you revisit your past and identify where your beliefs started, you will have a new awareness and clarity. It is common for habits to subside, insecurities to lift, and new healthier patterns to emerge. After identifying my limiting beliefs and eradicating them, my lifelong battle with food

———————————
* This process inspired and created by Rythmia Life Advancement Center.

ceased; I no longer overate, I could have snacks in the house, and I didn't obsess about food. Furthermore, my relationships with others changed. I was more present, more focused, and none of my experiences were tainted with beliefs of unworthiness anymore because I had learned that being alive is what makes us worthy. We are love and light and that is always enough.

Your outside world will change and improve when you heal your internal world.

When you go on these emotional healing journeys, you may try to trivialize your pain. So often we feel like our hurt is not enough, that we're overreacting or being dramatic. We think, *Yes I've been through a lot, but other people have been through so much more.* Downplaying our pain is another sneaky ego trick trying to get you to avoid feeling the emotions needed to heal for good. Don't let your ego manipulate you. Pain is pain, and for each person who experiences trauma, no matter how large or small, it feels life threatening. Don't let your ego try to tell you your pain is not worth feeling because others have it worse. And furthermore, don't let your sneaky fear-based mind try to tell you that you have so much trauma that you are broken and unfixable. The thing with trauma is it always hurts no matter what, everyone experiences it, and no matter how intense, what happened will go on to define us. It's time to return to the true us, and not be ruled by a singular event or painful experiences from our past. The only way to heal ourselves and connect back to our authentic self is to feel the pain we thought was impossible to process. When you feel it, you will heal it and you will transform your entire life.

The freedom that comes from knowing you aren't the things you used to think about yourself is the real reward and magic of it all. Imagine living your life in full connection to your authentic self—no more shadows, no more insecurities, no more habits, patterns, or self-abuse. Imagine truly knowing that you are perfect as you are, and your divinity is your worth.

The goal is to recognize your defining moment.

What beliefs have you developed because of it?

Who have you become as a result of this false-based belief system?

Give yourself permission to feel, for it is the only true path to heal.

Radical Recap

JOY BUSTER: Letting false beliefs shape your reality.

AWESOME OPPORTUNITY: Feel your feelings and focus on releasing them instead of suppressing them.

MANTRA: "I rise above my past and see all emotional pain as opportunities for growth."

The Big 5

——

RELEASE THE BELIEFS THAT YOU HAVE TO BE HAPPY AND JOYFUL ALL THE TIME

We are here to awaken from our illusion of separateness.

—THICH NHAT HANH

AT THIS POINT IN OUR journey together, I want to point out that Joy Seeking is not just a focus on *joy*. Creating your joy-filled life is not about seeking joy and being happy the entire time. It's about meaning, depth, and an authentic connection with ourselves and others. It's about living life as fully as possible. To be a Joy Seeker means you are committing to being present in each stage of your life. And that means breathing in the contrast and letting it fold into you. Seeking to feel good is important, but trying to completely escape not feeling good is avoiding life.

Many of us believe we have to be happy or joyful all the time, and if we aren't, then we are doing this life thing wrong.

We feel like sadness makes us deficient. We judge our feelings and ourselves for having them.

I used to believe that I needed to feel good and be happy all the time, and if I wasn't, then something was seriously wrong with me. Can you relate? I think this is common, especially if you've been on a personal growth path and you are practicing the tools. When we are investing in the programs, books, courses, coaching sessions, and so forth, but the results are unsatisfying, it can be easy to feel mad, frustrated, or disillusioned. We blame ourselves or the world. "What am I doing wrong?" "Why am I so off track?" Well you aren't off track at all. You feel this way because you are stuck in your head, in your belief that your life is supposed to look a different way than what it actually does. When our life doesn't look like what we think it should, we either go into a depression or feel anxious, or we fake it. That's right, we become masters at pretending things are okay. But manufacturing a false reality in which we can only be joyful, happy, and content is doing ourselves a disservice.

Some of my life coach friends do this. They do everything in their power to feel good. They put so much pressure on themselves to be happy. They believe feeling bad is . . . well, bad. If they aren't happy, they think they must be doing something wrong. They beat themselves up, feeling pressured to have a happy life, because they are the "experts" and should know how achieve it. So they focus on "living their best life" and avoiding anything negative.

On the outside this may seem like a great game plan, but their commitment to "feeling good" and only being around positive people or good things has a down side. When they feel low, they aren't honest with themselves or those around them. They deny their feelings and shut them out. But those feelings are valid, and sadness is part of life. They want so much to feel good and to practice what they preach but at a cost, because they are not embracing all that life has to offer.

In our friendships, I often feel like something is missing; the depth, the realness is not available to us because they are so focused on being and staying happy, they never want to share when they are not feeling good. They see it as a sign of weakness, a vulnerable part of them that they want to ignore and pretend isn't real. But real friendship is connection and trust, which is built on honesty, and when we avoid our feelings and don't express ourselves, the person we lie to the most is ourselves. When we aren't being honest with ourselves about how we feel, we can't grow connections with others, but most importantly we can't connect with our true self. Take this opportunity to become aware of where you may be lying to yourself. If you're not okay, it's okay.

When we try to feel good all the time we avoid deeper connections with others. This approach to life, "trying so hard to feel good all the time," comes at a price. It's not a club I want to participate in, and if you are reading this book, you too want more for your life. The *more* we crave is realness. It comes down to authenticity and being real with ourselves so we can connect with others.

Being real means allowing yourself to be human—and seeing that sadness and discomfort can be just as beautiful an experience as joy and happiness.

Our true self wants to feel it all. The human part of us needs this depth of life. Feeling frustrated, sad, and overwhelmed doesn't feel good, but there is a richness of life felt in these moments. The goal is not to avoid them but to be present with them and soon enough, when we do this, we can move through them and dance our way into a more balanced state.

Joy Jaunt: Feel Your Feelings

Next time you're feeling off, sad, depressed, frustrated, or mad, be present with yourself, love yourself through the experience, and be aware if you judge yourself for feeling these emotions. You can even repeat the mantra, "This isn't my forever state." Then ask yourself, "Why is this feeling here? What is this emotion trying to reveal to me?" Be fully in the feeling. If you're mad, let yourself be mad. If you're overwhelmed—acknowledge it. Then ask, "What steps can I do right now to move myself into a more balanced state?" The goal isn't to push the emotions away, but to be with them as you live your life. Let them coexist alongside you. They don't need to define you.

When you feel the raw emotions of life, instead of feeling bad for this, simply exist with them. Allow them to be part of your journey. As you do this, you can gracefully live your life more deeply. And that is the true essence of feeling connected to your authentic self. Because you soon see that joy is not a destination but a way of consciously living. We have to feel our emotions, give ourselves permission to be in them. Let them show you what needs to be expressed. When you feel your feelings, they feel understood, like a little child who needs acknowledgment. Then they will give you guidance into a deeper way of being. Sure, feeling good is amazing; it's what we strive for. But feeling unwell, sad, or frustrated can be liberating, too. It's part of living a balanced life that must not be avoided. There is beauty in our breakdowns, and the denser, darker emotions of life are just as valid, if not even more important to being alive, for in these uncomfortable moments we learn what it is we value most.

Believing we shouldn't be sad is a story our ego projects. Think about the stories, the ideas, the beliefs and habits you cling to. Most of the time because we believe in them so firmly, they shape our reality. The stories are the things we say to ourselves about ourselves and the world. It is our perspective and beliefs. I call them the sexy stories. The sexy story is our point of entry into the world, meaning our worldview is shaped by our own internal beliefs. Our habits, insecurities, even our fears all impact our perception of ourselves and the world. We create our own realities base on our beliefs and perceptions.

The key is to let go of the stories and the beliefs that are keeping you frustrated and stuck in life. We can learn how to recognize the stories and disengage from them. When we are stuck in the stories, it can feel debilitating. I use the word *stuck* intentionally because it feels like we can't move ahead or change our circumstances. No matter how hard we try, we feel like things aren't working out in our favor. This is because we believe that what we think is true, and we replay stories in our mind. If we perceive the world as harsh and we feel it is against us, then that is the reality we will live. If we feel disrespected and alone, it is because we are disrespecting ourselves.

When we are stuck in the stories, we treat ourselves poorly with negative thoughts and often even unhealthy and harmful habits. We can slowly disengage from the stories. When we do, we begin to move from being numb to life to feeling more accepting of our circumstances. When we are stuck in the stories, it's common to compare ourselves to others. We look at others and we think that we are worse off, which makes our pain even more difficult to bear. The stories we tell ourselves about ourselves, our circumstances, and the world are very real to us, but it is all an illusion. I want to help you step away from fear and step into a place of understanding. Consider that perhaps each situation in your life can be looked at in a new way. This will help you move into a place of possibilities rather than stay stuck in fear, denial, and shame.

In order to efficiently move past our stories, we need to identify the main ones holding us back. What do you tell yourself about yourself, and what do you say to yourself about life? Remember, these stories may seem very real to you and they likely have created your reality. For example, if you believe men are cheaters, then you may attract men who cheat on you. If you believe it's impossible to lose weight and you are doomed to be overweight forever, then it will be extremely hard to see the scale move. You have to tap into an unshakable confidence within yourself. When we believe in ourselves, we know we deserve and can have what we really want. Instead of thinking it's not going to work out for you, believe with every fiber of your body that life is working out in your favor, and you will soon see radical results.

The things we think become our lens through which we see the world. The thoughts we have are extremely important. They are powerful. The thoughts running through your mind can help to create the life of your dreams, or put you smack-dab in the middle of living some of your greatest fears.

At the fundamental level, thoughts are energy. Focusing your thoughts will help you live a more balanced life.

Whatever we think about or focus on consistently, we move toward.

Instead of the world happening to you, you will feel more empowered and see that everything is happening *for* you. One of the easiest ways to clear up your thoughts is to get clear about the stories you've been replaying and relying on to get you through life. I've gathered a list of the top stories we tell ourselves that are preventing us from moving forward into a more joyful life.

The 5 Big Stories We Tell Ourselves That Keep Us Stuck (and How to Transform Them)

Story 1: We need to feel good all the time

So many of us feel like something is wrong if we aren't happy. The pursuit of happiness can make us feel less than when we don't live up to its impossible standard. If you believe you should be happy all the time, then when you don't feel great, you will feel like a failure. But all feelings are part of the rich tapestry of life, and running away from any of them is not embracing life fully.

THE FIX: When you are sad and frustrated, recognize that they are valid feelings and just focus on being present. Let yourself exist with your feelings. When you can appreciate what is, you will move through it more efficiently.

Story 2: It's selfish to go after what we want

So many of us feel it is selfish to go for what we want; meanwhile we stay stuck, unhappy, and miserable. Think about the fact that the number one regret of the dying is, "I wish I had led a life more true to myself instead of what others wanted for me." Take steps now to be more true to yourself.

THE FIX: By actively pursuing your dreams, you not only lift up yourself but you help lift up the entire world. Because being authentic and living your truth is the only way you can fulfill your divine purpose.

Story 3: Life is supposed to look a certain way—I'll be happy when . . .

Everywhere we look, people seem to have more, be more, and look so much happier than we are. In our digital age, illusionary social media accounts make us feel bad about ourselves and pressure us to live up to their standards. We pretend to be better than we feel; we put a smile on our face; we overbuy, overeat, overwork, all in an effort to fit in. Meanwhile we are hurting inside, we are lonely, and we crave a deeper connection. We feel like our life is supposed to look a certain way, and if it doesn't match our vision, we feel off track and behind.

This story goes: Life is okay now, but it could be so much better, when you get the new car, lose the weight, get out of debt, get the new position, meet your soul mate—the list goes on and on. So many of us think when we get to the next level of our life, when we have the thing we think we need, only then can we be happy. This is a clever trick your ego plays on you to keep you safe and small. But your life isn't when something happens. It is happening right now.

THE FIX: Focus on the journey and all the amazing things happening in your life today. It's nice to have goals, but don't block yourself from living in the moment. Instead, celebrate your life today and be happy you are working toward more fulfillment.

Furthermore, instead of pretending that things are okay, be honest with yourself and share your true self. Be where you are instead of where you think you need to be. By being more true to yourself, you will feel better.

Story 4: What others think about me matters

So many of us make choices based on what other people think, say and do. We walk around feeling unworthy and trying to fit in, but we sacrifice ourselves and hide pieces of us in order to do this. We care so much about what others think; yet we don't stop to ask ourselves what *we* really think.

THE FIX: Realize that other people's opinion of you doesn't really matter, what matters most is your relationship with you. Practice self-love and self-compassion and take your attention off of needing others' approval, instead approve of yourself.

Story 5: Giving up is failure

In my retreats and workshops people ask me what the difference is between giving up and failing. Most of us think that giving up is failure and we hold on to situations, people, expenses, beliefs, and habits that don't serve us anymore. Believing that giving up is a bad thing is one habit that could be preventing you from feeling better.

THE FIX: Instead, shift your perception to see that we are always changing and growing. And often we outgrow what we once needed to grow into. You no longer need to be in the position, or with the person, or in the situation that is hurting your soul. Instead, give yourself permission to let go and move on. When you do, something more beautiful can emerge in its place.

> *When you transform the limiting stories that you believe, you transform your life.*

Look at this list of stories and identify the ones that have been keeping you stuck. Focus on the fix and trust that the stories you believe can be transformed into a more loving and positive focus.

Radical Recap

JOY BUSTER: Thinking you need to be happy all the time.

THE FIX: Show more of the real you in all aspects of your life. Be more vulnerable and accepting of yourself.

MANTRA: "I awaken from the illusions that separate me from love."

The Priceless Point

————

RELEASE THE NEED TO KNOW THE OUTCOME

Expectations are resentments waiting to happen.
—Brené Brown

ANOTHER STORY WE TELL OURSELVES is that the outcome matters most. If I do X and Y it will give me Z. But when Z doesn't happen we fall into guilt and shame. In fact this story—that the goal, the outcome, is the most important thing—deserves its own section.

I have a good friend who called me really upset after yet another failed first date. She said, "Over the years, I've invested thousands of dollars in books, courses, and retreats, all on how to get the man. I am almost forty and still single. I'm alone and wondering why I've wasted so much money, time, and energy." I understood her frustration, but I could see her focus on what she didn't have was keeping her from seeing the potential. She was too focused on the outcome, which made her feel like she was doing it wrong. When we fixate on a specific outcome, it can rob us of accessing joy in the moment. She spent money on trying to find her soul mate, and because she hasn't found him yet, she feels like a failure. But what about all she learned? What about all the experiences she has had? What about all the other wonderful things in her life?

I coached a client who was also a full-time world traveler. She reached out for support because she was contemplating ending her trip early. I asked her what the problem was, why was she so worried about ending the trip early. She said, "It would all be a waste; I've put time, money, energy, and focus into this dream, and if it doesn't turn out the way I thought, then it's a waste." But this was a perspective keeping her stuck. We worked together to uncover that everything she had invested was actually part of her growth, and because she took those steps, she became more of who she really is. And the real her doesn't want to be a full-time world traveler anymore. She had to let go of "the story" in order to grow and move on.

Can you relate to these stories? Maybe you've spent a lot of time, money, or energy in a situation hoping for a specific outcome, but the outcome you are in is not what you hoped for. You may have gotten angry with yourself, resentful of others, and angry at the world. However, have you ever considered you just have to change course and your perspective? We have to give ourselves permission to be who we truly are and that means honoring the process. But we can't do this if we are expecting specific outcomes. You may think things seem to be off track, but you will soon see that life is actually going right and you are closer than you've ever been to getting what you need. The universe is always giving us what we need. When we focus exclusively on one outcome, we tend to get tunnel vision and lose sight of all the other benefits we are receiving. We miss the present moment and the amazing things unfolding in front of us. Brené Brown said, "Joy comes to us in ordinary moments. We risk missing out when we get too busy chasing down the extraordinary."

Think about your own life and the outcomes you are expecting. The ideal number on the scale, a ring on the finger, a certain number in your bank account? Why are you waiting on happiness? Why not allow yourself right now to feel it, give yourself permission to be happy, and connect to joy before these goals are reached?

I have another friend who for much of her life has been focused on losing weight. She counts every calorie, avoids social situations that involve eating out, and refuses to have her photo taken until she hits her goal weight. She avoids things she loves like pasta and pizza in a quest to hit a specific number on the scale, and most of our conversations revolve around what she can and can't eat. I asked her what will happen when she hits the goal weight. She said she will finally be able to relax and be happy. She's placed her happiness in a specific outcome, and this mentality is a choice. She doesn't have to feel guilty for eating food now, but she believes this is the cause of her unhappiness. I used to feel just like her, so I know the pressure we can feel as we try to control things in our life hoping to feel happiness when we reach our goal. But the guilt I felt and the guilt my friend feels is not because of the food. It is because we are denying ourselves what we really want. Many of us feel shame because we aren't fully living our life. We are avoiding the richness of life. I got to a place in my own journey where I was sick of counting calories and avoiding foods I really loved. I didn't want the scale to decide my worth, so I stopped feeling guilty and started to enjoy life more. As I did, my relationship with food, with myself, and with others improved. It's all a choice. We get to choose how we want to live. I decided life is too short to feel guilty for just being alive, so I changed my focus from lack, shame, and guilt, to love, abundance, and joy. We always have a choice.

The expectations we have are the things that are hurting us. Instead of receiving the outcome in order to think it's all worth it, see each investment as a stepping-stone. And as the Chinese proverb says, *The journey is the reward.*

The value you get along the way is so much more important than the outcome.

I asked my friend who was dating what value she's been getting by investing in these programs and books to find true love, and as she sniffled her tears away she said, "Well, I am more clear about what I don't want, I love myself now more than I ever have, and I have more respect for myself now than I did before." This is priceless. "Yes!" I said. "That is the priceless point and not a waste at all." We think we want a specific outcome, but the lessons we learn along the way and the personal growth are far more important. Relax a little more, release expectations, and be in the journey. Stop thinking things are a waste or you've messed up, because when you trust yourself and listen to your heart, you are always right where you are supposed to be.

Radical Recap

> **JOY BUSTER:** Believing we are off track or behind because the outcome we wanted doesn't match our current reality.

THE FIX: Be more in the journey and see your situation as a reward.

MANTRA: "My life is a constant unfolding. I focus on accepting what is instead of wishing for what isn't."

Replace Worry
With Wonder

RELEASE WORRY

*Worry never robs tomorrow of its sorrow, it
only saps today of its joy.*

—Leo F. Buscaglia

RECENT STUDIES HAVE ESTIMATED THAT 86 percent of
adults classify themselves as worriers—and they can
spend almost up to two hours doing it every day! That's nearly
twenty-eight days a year spent on worry. I used to worry a lot.
It was my go-to form of existence. I worried about my weight,
what others would think about me, what others would say,
my lifestyle choices, the direction of my life. It seemed my entire day was full of worry. In my last book *The Self-Love
Experiment*, I talk about my journey to self-love, and learning
to disengage with the worry mind is one of the best ways to
do that. I want to go deeper into this concept here.

When we are worried, we can't focus on what we want,
or see the truth of our situation, because we are too con-

sumed with fear. When we worry it is because we are trying to protect ourselves from being blindsided. Worry, like
fear, is also in our life to tell us something. If we already
think about the worst-case outcome and that bad situation
happens, then we can be more prepared. It's an ego mind
trick. If it happens we will be in more control, and this situation was planned for. This is a protection mechanism our
brains create, but most of the time we don't know that
worry is hindering us. The worst-case scenarios hardly
ever happen, so when we trust our worry, we just keep ourselves stuck in fear. Now, instead of worrying, replace your
fear with wonder. Wonder is opportunity, playfulness, and
exploration. Every time my mind falls into worry, I catch
myself and turn it into a wonder statement. It looks something like this:

Joy Jaunt: Turn Your Worry into Wonder

WORRY: What if I fail and it doesn't work out?

WONDER: What if it goes better than planned, and I
am happier than I ever thought I could be?

WORRY: What if people don't understand or approve
of what I do?

WONDER: What if people love it and my idea is well
received?

WORRY: What if I get rejected?

WONDER: What if I get accepted? My life will change
for the better.

WORRY: What if I am never accepted or loved for
who I am?

WONDER: What would it be like to become my own
best friend?

Try it out for yourself. What is your biggest worry? What
consumes your mind? Instead of worrying, turn it into a wonder statement. The goal is to retrain your brain to focus on
the good. As you do this, it will become habitual to focus on
the good and overcome the anxiety associated with worry.

Radical Recap

JOY BUSTER: Worrying, overanalyzing, thinking too
much.

THE FIX: Instead of focusing on what you don't want,
focus on what you do want.

MANTRA: "I celebrate all that could go right; everything
is in divine order."

You Can't Bypass the Sponge Phase

——

RELEASE THE IDEA THAT THERE IS ONLY
ONE RIGHT WAY TO DO THINGS

Don't judge each day by the harvest you reap,
but by the seeds that you plant.
— ROBERT LOUIS STEVENSON

THINK ABOUT YOUR OWN CURIOSITIES and what brings you immense joy. Maybe you have a passion for something, and dream about being able to spend more time doing it. Maybe you even want to make a living sharing your knowledge about it. Maybe you don't really have a dream, but you want to be able to accept where you are or be happy with yourself. Well, this itself is a desire that wants to be reached. We get insights or nudges all the time about what we want and don't want. It is important to trust these nudges. Honor the curious moments and trust they are pulling you into what is meant for you.

Once I removed my limiting beliefs and transformed my stories, I started to get insights that I wanted to be a writer.

Right after I left the corporate world, I began to feel curious about the publishing industry. I read books on how to become a travel writer. I took online classes on how to become a published author and secure a literary agent. I spent hours in bookstores looking at book covers and titles, seeing how authors and publishing houses set up content. I call this the *sponge phase*. We soak up information and absorb all we can about the topics that interest us.

Immerse yourself in the study of you. Treat your curiosity like a job. Take classes, buy books, talk to people about what you are learning, because all of this is part of the process of you connecting to your authentic self. Each step, one step at a time, will pull you forward.

I have a friend who runs her own home goods company. She has a full-time job in the day and dedicates her evening hours to creating and selling products that bring people joy. Her vision is to eventually leave her corporate job and run her own company full-time. I called her the other day while she was at a home goods trade show, one of the nation's largest retail buyer conferences. For years it was her dream to have a booth at such a big show, so potential retail buyers could feature her products in their stores across America. I was so excited to talk to her during the event because I knew how important this goal was for her. To be featured in this show is a really big deal as it puts her in front of top buyers in the retail industry. I was expecting to hear a happy, thrilled friend. After all her dream had come true—she made it to the show, right? But our dreams hardly ever turn out the way we expect, which is why it is important to release the expectation and instead focus on the experience of the dream. When we talked, I heard the stress and anxiety in her voice. She was at the show, but it was nothing like what she thought. The entire process was like a new language she needed to learn. By coming to the conference, she learned that in order to get to the next level she had a lot she still needed to learn. So when we talked, she was overwhelmed, stressed, tired, and the first thing she said was, "I haven't sold anything." I could tell she was disappointed, smack-dab in the middle of her big dream, and she still hadn't gotten what she thought she came for—sales. She thought she was going to sell a bajillion of her products and be big time right away, hopefully get picked up by a big retail chain like Anthropologie or Urban Outfitters, then voilà, instant fame and her product in stores across the nation. We all want that instant magic bullet, fast track to success, right? But the opposite was happening: She wasn't being approached; she felt out of place and like she was clueless about the process. But she had to show up for this part of her life. She had to arrive at this conference in order to learn the steps needed to manifest her bigger goal, the ideal life she was trying to create. We have to dive fully into the steps and release our expectations. You see, she thought she was going to sell product, but the universe knew she needed to learn key steps to getting to the level where she could sell product to large chain retailers. It was clear the moment she arrived that the reason she thought she was coming and the reason she was really there were very different. But that doesn't mean she was off track at all. In fact, this was a critical stepping-stone in manifesting her ideal life.

We may not always get what we want, but the universe knows what we truly need.

I asked her if she was glad that she came, and she said, "I wouldn't change this for the world. The amount of learning I am getting is indispensable. It's like a masterclass in what I need to know. I am on warp speed here with a glimpse into my future." This is the sponge phase and we can't bypass it. We learn the way on the way, and the sponge phase is essential to our progression forward. The sponge phase is everything because it is where we learn what we need to learn in order to get what we want most: freedom, joy, security, and love.

You can't just wake up one day and reach your goal, because we have to become the person who can receive what we want. It is the process that counts for the true joy. Everyone goes through it. We can't escape it, for it is part of growing into who you are meant to be. But the sponge phase is very different for every single person, because the Universe gives you the specific lessons that you need for your own soul's growth. Don't compare your journey to someone else's, even if you are in the same industry. We all have specific things we need to learn, patterns we need to heal. It's all part of our journey.

Part of my sponge phase was letting go of how my writing career should look. I assumed to be a successful author you needed a partnership with the same publisher. But every single book I've written so far (the past four) have been with different publishers. That's four books, four different publishers. This used to really frustrate me because I took it personally. I thought it meant they didn't like me or think I was a good enough author to keep on their team. I thought if they didn't buy my next book idea it meant I was off track or behind. The truth is there were all kinds of factors that had nothing to do with me that went into the decision to not sign me again. I now know my thoughts and worries were ego projections, fear and insecurities in my head. They were all silly stories. One day I was out with my brother explaining my frustration that every book is with a different publisher, and he looked at me with an odd face and said, "Seems silly you are worrying about that." I said, "What do you mean?" He replied, "Well, seems like as long as you get to do what you want making the amount of money you want, then that's success." I realized how right he was. My perspective shifted immediately.

Today, I know the truth. My heart knows that having different publishers has nothing to do with me as a writer and my potential for fulfillment. The shift for me was when I turned to gratitude that I actually had four books out in the world. "I am so thankful I get to do what I love and reach people with my message. How amazing that *I get to* experience different publishers." You see a completely different perspective, one that feels much better, joyful, and expansive.

In the beginning of my career, I was a nervous wreck pitching my books because I tied my worth to the outcome. But something changed once I dived into writing this one. I learned how to release my fear and instead place my focus on faith. The sponge phase gave me the gift of arriving at a place where I no longer stress, because I believe so fully in myself and my work and the unfolding process of being who you are meant to be. Now I see life as a creative journey and an ongoing exploration.

Your path looks nothing like anyone else's. Neither does mine. It's important to trust your own journey. You are always on the best path for you. Turn to gratitude for whatever you're going through, because most often it is for your highest good.

Radical Recap

JOY BUSTER: Thinking that there is only one way to succeed.

AWESOME OPPORTUNITY: Trust your own path and focus on your own unfolding plan.

MANTRA: "I trust the process and know that I am on my own journey."

Joy Seeker Journal Time

In your workbook or joy journal, take a moment to answer the following questions before progressing to the next section.

- What story have I been believing that is no longer serving me?
- How can I replace my worry with wonder?
- What can I let go of that no longer feels good?
- What breakthrough have I been looking for and how has it kept me from being present?

Anything can
happen.
The unfolding
is where the
magic is!

"I AM ROOTED IN THE NOW"
"I LOOK FORWARD TO THE
UNIVERSE SURPRISING ME."

#JoySeeker

— YOU —

GET TO

Decide

YOUR VIBE

#JoySeeker

PART 3

THE BECOMING

How to Embrace What Is While Creating What Could Be

What You Want Wants You, Too

EMBRACE YOUR DESIRES

Everything you want is out there waiting for
you to ask. Everything you want also wants you.
But you have to take action to get it.

—JACK CANFIELD

SO MANY OF US FEEL like we have to become something more than what we are. We need to be richer, smarter, prettier, taller, thinner, healthier, more popular, more of anything than our real self. This constant feeling of not being quite good enough overshadows our actions. We are afraid to go after what we really want because secretly we feel like we don't deserve it. But all that changes when we recognize we can decide our vibe. The next phase of our journey is about knowing that you are enough and deserve to live a joy-filled, happy life. And in this newfound clarity you will feel more alive and connected to your true self. In this exciting space, anything is possible for you and your loved ones.

Each phase of our life is a constant unfolding as we grow and learn more about ourselves. Think of yourself like an onion. We have layers to us, and each time we reveal a new layer we can peel it back to discover more of our core essence. But our base, the core of us, is always there. When people say you've changed, you're really just becoming more of who you really are. It's an evolution of your own personal growth, your soul's own journey.

Many of those layers that cover our core are our fears, beliefs, and insecurities. Naturally, when we let go of these fears and release the worry we can see our true self more clearly. One of the easiest ways to let go of the layers that have blocked us is by focusing more on what we want. And I don't just mean that one thing, like finding your soul mate, getting that promotion, or finally getting along with your daughter-in-law. I mean the essence of your desires. If you are honest with yourself, it is so much bigger than that one thing you think you want.

I thought traveling the world for a full year was my dream, and it was. But what I really wanted was what traveling the world represented. It was freedom, financial freedom, exploration, and a lifestyle that supported self-discovery and being of service to others. I wanted to connect with purpose and feel a sense of belonging. I was traveling because I was in search of a feeling. I was trying to find the place that I belonged. I wanted to fit, I wanted to feel content, in a world that often made me feel less than. What I wanted was peace. What I was in search of was joy.

So many of us are looking for that *feeling* to make us feel more connected to ourselves and others. We travel through life in search of these feelings, the ones that might help us move forward, but when we aren't clear about what we are actually looking for, the search will be endless. Most of the time, because we aren't certain, we chase things outside of ourselves for ways to feel better.

What we need to do is carve out moments for thoughtful reflection so we can invite our true self, our intuition, and our divine guidance in. It is in this space of reflection that we can allow ourselves to be inspired from within. In order to find out what it is you're really seeking on this journey, you need to tap into your deepest needs and open yourself up to new possibilities, allow yourself to dream, and get a crystal-clear vision of your ideal life.

Once we have stripped away our fears and limiting beliefs, once we have become more focused, clear, and connected to our higher self, and once we have identified our true needs, we have to invite what we need into our life. You may have heard of the Law of Attraction and you may have read books like *The Secret* by Rhonda Byrne or *You Are a Badass* by Jen Sincero, or any text from Abraham and Jerry and Esther Hicks, all law of attraction books (at the end of this book I've included a resource section that lists some of my favorite books on this subject). The Law of Attraction is based on the principle that everyone and everything is made up of energy and has a vibration or frequency, and that like attracts like. It's the belief that by focusing on positive or negative thoughts, we put out positive or negative energy and thus bring positive or negative experiences into our life. But if you've never heard of it or don't quite understand it yet, trust that you've been working with this law whether you realize it or not. One way to see it in action is to look at your life and think about the things that are not going well. Then ask yourself, "What have I been thinking about this situation?" Have you been focusing on how it won't work out, how you aren't where you want to be, or how it's making you so unhappy? On the flip side, think about what is going well in your life and what your thoughts around those situations have been. Positive thoughts will create beautiful results. If this is what you've been focusing on in your mind, then most likely this is the outcome you are experiencing. The law of attraction is a powerful principle that can make our life amazing and joyful.

Once you start harnessing the power of your own energy, everything starts to shift in beautiful ways for you.

The problem is, most people are focused on what they don't want. They think about it, worry about it, they're afraid of it. These negative thoughts create negative energy, and then we wonder why we keep getting what we don't want. When we understand and practice the law, we can shift our attention to focus on what we want, because ultimately it wants us, too. Start to think in terms of desires, possibilities, and expansion rather than being stuck, depleted, and constricted.

Esther Hicks, one of my favorite spiritual teachers, shared in her book *The Law of Attraction: The Basics of the Teachings of Abraham*, that "To better understand the Law of Attraction, see yourself as a magnet attracting unto you the essence of that which you are thinking and feeling. And so, if you are feeling fat, you cannot attract thin. If you feel poor, you cannot attract prosperity, and so on. It defies Law."

No matter where you are right now, you can step into your ideal life. But it starts 100 percent with your vibe. Start by putting your own energy into feeling better. I used to be very tense. I was anxious and worried all the time. But once I started harnessing the Law of Attraction, focusing on and visualizing what

I wanted and how I wanted to feel, things began to shift. I felt more calm, focused, and present. Things I wanted came to me with so much more ease.

Welcome to the real you. The real you does not need to struggle, feel stuck, or feel frustrated. The real you lives in joy, peace, and harmony. Harnessing the power of good energy is rewarding because the real you gets to connect to

In order for things to change in your life, you have to see things as you want them, not as they are.

your heart center and dive deeper into who you really are. Understand that if everything is energy and has its own frequency, then the things we want have an energy to them, too. So essentially you want to be in a vibrational match to your desires. Someone who has found their life purpose, met their soul mate, is pursuing their dreams, and has connected to their true self has an energy that is very different from someone who talks down to themselves, complains about everything or replays negative thoughts, and feels off track and behind. It's about being what you want to attract, because this will bring what you want to you much faster.

Joy Jaunt: Be What You Want to Attract

Think about your desires. What do you want, and what energy would be exuded by someone who already has what you want?

How can you move yourself into this same vibration? What does your ideal life feel like, what is the vibe? And how would someone who has that life act, be, behave? Focus on the feeling more than the actual thing. Let the feelings guide you.

When I was planning my trip around the world, the insecure part of me wasn't sure I could pull it off. But I practiced the Law of Attraction. I started to act like a person who has the confidence to travel the globe solo. What qualities does a world traveler have? What is their outlook on life? How do they see the world and themselves? How do they make smart, budget-friendly travel choices? Instead of letting my pesky fear stop me, I vibrated myself into being the essence of a world traveler and soon enough I was off on my journey living the exact same vibration of my vision. Try it out yourself. If what you want isn't here yet, how would someone who has what you want act, feel, and be? To become what we want, we must first become it with our energy and focus.

> *There is no separation between all that you want, and all you truly are.*

Radical Recap

Your desires are important. When you focus on the feeling and essence of what you want it can come to you faster.

AWESOME OPPORTUNITY: Focus on what you want with positive thoughts and energy. Be what you want to attract.

MANTRA: "What I want wants me, too."

Your Health on Happiness

EMBRACE WELL-BEING

*Much of our pain or misery in life stems from
our own outlook towards the situation. A para-
lyzed person can also be happy, so can be a
financially poor family.*

—AMIT AHLAWAT

I USED TO WORK WITH SOMEONE who was, without a doubt, the most negative person I'd ever met. Every single thing out of her mouth was a judgment, complaint, negative perspective or putdown about herself, about others, and how she saw the world. She never said one nice thing about anything or anyone. She would bring up grudges from decades ago, feelings she was harboring about her family and past coworkers; this woman never let anything go. Her energy was always super frantic. Every time we would work together, I would leave the meeting feeling funky. I never put two and two together until one time I actually felt nauseous after a long meeting with her. It was so bad, I had to go lie down. I thought to myself, *Could her negativity and extremely harsh outlook be affecting my own health?* It may sound silly, but according to the Law of Attraction, science and psychology, this could be very possible. Other people's mental or emotional state can affect us.

What we believe can also affect our health and those around us. And a harsh outlook and constant negative perception can harm our physical bodies if we aren't careful. The Law of Attraction is about behavior and action but also about how you think and your beliefs. You may have heard of the placebo effect; the medical community has proven that when patients in clinical trials get nothing but sugar pills, saline injections, or fake surgeries but *believe* they might be getting the new wonder drug or miracle surgery, their bodies get better 18 to 80 percent of the time. Lissa Rankin, author of *Mind Over Medicine: Scientific Proof That You Can Heal Yourself*, writes about the *nocebo effect*, which means the opposite is true—that negative beliefs about our health or harsh care from insensitive doctors can indeed harm the body if we believe it.

> *Our negative beliefs will manifest the outcome we don't want.*

Now I'm not suggesting that people should be blamed for every illness they get, that they are responsible for their disease. Nor am I saying that positive belief is the only factor to overcome illness. I know fully the power of using all modalities available to us when healing. But we can't deny the role negative thoughts play in our own well-being. As Lissa Rankin explains in her *mindbodygreen* article, "Scientific Proof That Negative Beliefs Harm Your Health,"

"Obviously, accidents happen, genetic risk factors influence our health, and bad things happen to good people with positive thoughts. But these studies show that, even in light of these things we can't always prevent, what we believe, especially what we fear, has a tendency to manifest itself in reality because negative beliefs fill our bodies with harmful cortisol and epinephrine, while positive beliefs relax our nervous systems and allow our bodies to heal." Ask yourself how your beliefs may be helping or hurting your health. Do you believe you'll be on meds for the rest of your life? Are you resigned to the prognosis your doctor gave you? Do you focus on what is bad about the world or do you look for the good? Are you motivated to try to activate your own light, by shifting your beliefs from negative ones to positive ones? What you believe and focus on has an impact on everything in your life, especially your health. A good example of how your thoughts can help to heal you is Kris Carr, the wellness activist and *New York Times* bestselling author. She was diagnosed with cancer, and instead of listening to what the world was telling her to do, she turned inward to trust her inner guide. She looked inside herself for answers about how to eat and what to do and started to focus on positive thoughts and mantras inspired by Louise Hay's book *You Can Heal Yourself*. Decades later she is a cancer thriver with a huge online community of wellness warriors all choosing to focus on positive thoughts and healthy ways to heal from the inside out.

What does all of this mean for us? Well, if you're someone whose subconscious mind is filled with negative thoughts about yourself or others and limiting beliefs from your childhood, like "They were mean to me and I am unlovable"; "I'll never lose weight, because obesity runs in the family";

"Things never work out for me"; or "I'm never going to get better," you may be keeping yourself from the very things you want.

Radical Recap:

What you think and focus on affects your health.

AWESOME OPPORTUNITY: Think positive thoughts for positive results.

MANTRA: "I am well, all is well."

Your Universal Helpers are on Standby

EMBRACE SUPPORT

The Universe is saying: "Allow me to flow through you unrestricted, and you will see the greatest magic you have ever seen."

—KLAUS JOEHLE

SOMETIMES OUR JOY CAN ELUDE us because we are trying to do too much on our own. But asking for help is not a weakness, for it will give you strength. You can ask a friend or family member to help support you, but there is another kind of support available to us all the time. I learned that in order to move forward in life, we cannot do it on our own. I had to tap into a power greater than myself. You may call it goodness, goddess, the Universe, source energy, higher power, intuition, angels, gut feeling, true self, the vortex, Allah, Buddha, God, your higher self—what you identify with isn't as important as the feeling you get when you tap into this source energy. You can turn to prayer or meditation;

however you do it, accessing that energy source is the key to feeling better. I am talking about love energy. It is that energy that vibrates your truth. Nothing in the world feels as good as this connection because this source energy is who you are at your core—it is the natural loving state from which we are born. When we are connected to divine source energy, it feels good because it is real.

What we don't always think about is that this vibration is around us all the time. There is infinite support available to guide you—always. Many of us are closed off from this source of support because we can't see it, and we don't believe what we can't see. But I invite you to be open to feeling it. This energy is part of us, it is within us, *we* are the source energy, *we* are the love. And this love wants to support you. When we start to understand this, we see examples of this displayed in all areas of our life. I call them Universal helpers, and they are at your service.

When I arrived in Puerto Vallarta, Mexico, I had just come off a sixteen-hour trip from Costa Rica. I had slept on the airport floor in Mexico City because of a canceled flight (not fun, I know), and I was tired, overwhelmed, and frustrated. I arrived extremely hungry and delirious from all the airport changeovers. When my taxi driver dropped me off, he sped off quickly only for me to realize I was in the completely wrong neighborhood. There I was totally lost, super jet-lagged, and feeling like calling it quits. With no cell service, a fatigued body and mind, I was at the end of my emotional rope, wondering what all of the traveling was for. I sat down on the sidewalk in the middle of a deserted, dusty, neighborhood, put my head into my hands, and cried. I told myself that this idea of traveling the world wasn't at all worth it. I started to focus solely on all the bad things that were happening. My ego, fear-based mind was taking over, which often happens when we are tired and disconnected from our bigger purpose. Although my mind vigorously entertained the idea of calling it quits, I knew at this stage this wasn't an option. So I turned to a power greater than me, and I asked the Universe for help. When we ask our higher power for help, we will always get guidance to move us forward. I said, "Please help me, I feel so alone and lost. Please give me a sign this is all worth it." Within moments a Mexican woman in her sixties came over and leaned into my space, blocking the blazing sun. She asked if I was okay. I told her I was lost, and she picked me up with a gentle hug and brought me into her home a few feet away. She gave me a cold bottle of water and a towel to wipe away my sweat and tears. I showed her the map, but I was confused because I didn't know where we were, and without hesitation she grabbed her car keys and said in her broken English, "I will take you." At first I told her *no, please, no worries*, but she insisted. As we were driving over to the correct location, we couldn't communicate with words because of the language barrier, but we were speaking the universal language of love and support. She was taking care of a total stranger, and I was allowing myself to receive. It was in that moment I saw that she was my answered prayer. She was my sign, my universal support system sent to me as a reminder: It's all okay, and you are not alone.

After driving me to the correct neighborhood about ten minutes away, I offered to give her money, but she refused. She smiled brightly and said, "*No problemo.*" As I exited her car, I knew that she was my earth angel, sent by my Universal helpers. She was the guidance, the support, and friendly reminder from the Universe that I am safe and secure and we are always looked after.

The Universe sends us helpers all the time. They come in the form of people, ideas, conversations, songs, concepts, coaches, messages, videos, and books. We just need to be open to receiving the support. We all have Universal helpers. You have an energetic support system on standby ready to support and uplift you. I like to call them the band of angels. God, the Universe, your higher self (including your ancestors and archangels) are looking out for your best interest. When we feel alone, off track, stuck, or feel like calling it quits, we just simply need to remind ourselves that we are never alone and our support system is rooting for us. Don't forget the support is always there to guide you.

We are all connected to a limitless power of support and energy, but most of us aren't even using a fraction of it.

Although the Universal support system is always there, it's like a wise friend. It won't really help unless you ask. Our Universal helpers are on standby; they are waiting for the invitation to help. It is no coincidence that as soon as I reached out to ask for help, the woman showed up. I had to make the first move, the request, then my wish was given. Your Universal helpers want nothing more than to help you, so invite them often. When you feel stuck or want more clarity, reach out to the energetic support through prayer, meditation, journaling, or submersing yourself in nature, and ask for what you would like. The support system will always guide you forward. You can even do what I did and ask for the source energy to give you a sign. This is a powerful way to develop a deeper connection with your own internal guidance system and intuition.

The more you trust it and listen to it, the more balanced your life will be. You will feel an inner power that is your authentic truth. A knowing that comes from you being in alignment with who you are at your soul level.

Joy Jaunt: Get More Support

Dedicate some time today to developing your relationship with your Universal helpers. Pray, journal, meditate, or go into nature. Ask a specific question, such as, *What am I afraid of?* or *What message do you have for me?* And listen gently to the insights that come to you. The feelings and observations that follow are part of your guidance system. They will give you clarity and a path forward. The insights you receive will help support you on your journey. You can also use this time to ask your Universal support system to open up opportunities for more joy, abundance, even self-acceptance. This loving energy will support you with all of your needs and desires.

You may notice, I use the words *Universal source energy*, and *your true self* interchangeably. It's all divine love, so really there is no separation. This love is within you and you are an expression of this divinity. When we are connected to this love, we are in a state of flow, we are joyful, happy, and free. We feel connected to our best self and others, and we are open for inspiration and opportunities to come our way. When you are not connected to this energy, you may feel resistance, fear, jealousy, and anger. The goal is to move ourselves into feeling good and being in a state of flow because that is our truth. After you release your negative beliefs and stories, it is much easier to navigate yourself into a feel-good vibration. When you do this, you start to live your life in accordance with your true self.

Your intuition is the strongest tool you have in connecting to your true self. It is your own compass and you can always trust it.

One of the main ways I started to feel more connected to myself and my life was by shifting my focus. Instead of trying to do it all on my own, I started to lean on the Universal support to help me. It was so much easier! The more you rely on your Universal support system and practice the Law of Attraction, the more peaceful you will feel, your worry will be replaced with wonder and your fears will be replaced with love. The most beautiful part of tapping into this support system is that instead of limitations, you will start to live in possibilities. You will relax into your journey because you have a faith that extends beyond what you can see, as you trust your place in the world and yourself.

Radical Recap

There is a Universal support system—people, energy, and resources available to support and guide you forward. You just have to ask for help and be willing to receive.

AWESOME OPPORTUNITY: Use this support more often and develop a relationship with the universal support.

MANTRA: "Asking for help is not a weakness but a strength, for we all need each other to grow."

I've Got Friends in Other Glorious Places

EMBRACE SOUL SISTERS AND MISTERS

*Friends change…friendships change. Real
friends move with these changes and talk about
them as they are happening.*

—ANNE WILSON SCHAEFT

THE EXCITING PART OF ALL this is that feeling better and creating a life you want is 100 percent in your hands. This can be empowering when we understand all the tools available to us. Once you start using these tools, you will see a shift in your life. You will start to feel better and make healthier choices for you and loved ones. You will start to see the things that are not serving you will have a low-feeling vibration. They won't resonate with you anymore because you are raising your vibration, and you will want to shift away from things that don't feel good. As you honor this process, you soon see life becomes more gracious and easier. The struggle you once felt is replaced with wonder, peace, and awe. Give yourself permission to let go of things that no longer work in your life: people, places, situations, habits, dreams, thoughts, situations. Focus on what you can let go of. A woman I met at a meditation retreat described this perfectly. She said, "It's like you're a puzzle, and you learn and grow and your piece changes. And when you go back to your old puzzle, you oddly don't fit. It doesn't work anymore, so you have to find your new puzzle. You have to allow yourself to grow."

We will often outgrow what we once needed to grow into. Don't be afraid to let go.

Obviously, the more support you have in your life, the easier it is to enjoy your entire life. But sometimes we feel stuck because of the people we surround ourselves with. There's a concept called mirror neurons that explains how the people around you profoundly affect you. Have you ever wondered why you suddenly feel the urge to yawn when you see someone else yawn? This is because a neuron in your brain is mirroring what it observes. When you see someone smile, you smile, too, and you often feel a boost in your mood. This is why our favorite TV shows have laugh tracks; they're making the viewers laugh along, too. There are neurons in our brain that mirror what we see. If you are around someone who is constantly negative—picking at you, judging you and everyone else, complaining and focusing on what isn't working—the more you are around them, the more you will pick up and mirror these behaviors. We mirror each other without even realizing it. This happens on a subconscious level. This is also why it's extremely difficult to break generations of thought patterns. If your mother told you you would never amount to anything, or a sister told you your talent is worthless, you will mirror the beliefs and patterns. Motivational speaker Jim Rohn famously said that we are the average of the five people we spend the most time with.

On the flip side, if you spend your time with positive people, friends who inspire you, motivate, and encourage you, you are likely to feel more passionate about your own life and well-being. Protect your peace and surround yourself with people who are uplifting, joyful, and supportive. Sometimes our low energy and mood has nothing to do with us but the people we are around. By examining your social circle, you will be able to see if it is sucking the joy out of you.

Joy Jaunt: Take a Friendship Inventory

Identify the top five people you spend your time with. How do they make you feel? Do they uplift you, inspire you, and bring you joy? If not, how can you seek out new friends who are more supportive and kinder to you?

What happens for most of us is, as we start to learn new principles, ideas, and spiritual tools to help us grow and we start to feel much better, we want everyone around us to come along on this fabulous journey. We've found the pot of gold at the end of the rainbow and we want to share it with the world. But often our enthusiasm is met with resistance. We tell our friends and family about the books we are reading or the new dreams we have. We may even show up more authentically on social media, but the people who are in our life are scratching their heads saying, "Huh, who is this person? I don't recognize them." And you're thinking, *Well, this is the real me. I feel better than I ever have*, and you can't understand why everyone else isn't as excited as you are.

I remember when I first entered this new and exciting yet confusing phase. I had just left corporate and was diving head-first into my own self-awareness journey. I had just finished Gabrielle Bernstein's first book. I loved it so much, I bought five copies to give my closest friends. I was so excited to be giving this gift to help us all grow together. I hoped we could start a book club, and I imagined us all sitting around sharing concepts from the book and talking about our ideal life while we crafted our vision boards. But that fantasy was shattered when they unwrapped their presents. Instead of excitement, I just got blank stares. Then they all smiled at me warily as if I had three heads. That's when I realized my joy was clearly not everyone else's. And just because I was on a personal growth journey didn't mean those around me were, too.

I didn't know it at the time, but this is actually very common and is part of the growth process. To step fully into our true self so we can live the life we are meant to live we need to let go of what no longer serves us. And when the people in our life, sometimes those closest to us, best friends, even those we are in romantic relationships with, don't understand us anymore, it can feel lonely. It is as if we are speaking a foreign language and our newfound happiness and the clarity we have is intimidating to them. They just want things to be the same, old, comfortable, normal. But you are on a path of growth and that means new ideas, new thoughts, and new awareness. And once you start feeling better, you can never go back to who you were because you no longer belong there. This can cause added stress and more pressure to your life, but only if you are attached to keeping things the way they were. You can still love the people in your life but instead of needing them to change, simply seek out more like-minded people elsewhere.

When I left my corporate job to follow my dream to become a writer, one of my best friends—someone who was more like a sister to me—was so confused and hurt by my transformation. She couldn't understand why I wanted to write personal development books and she hated feel-good quotes I posted on my social media. Our conversations were always fueled with judgment and I felt her lack of support. Our friendship faded and we stopped talking. It was clear I was growing in a new direction, one that felt aligned with who I really was, and she was in a different vibration. The more me I showed, the more resistance I got. I finally let go of this friendship (because it felt toxic, it was keeping me from growing) and trusted that I was doing the right thing because I was being true to myself. After all, you don't want people around you who make you feel bad for being you. Although letting go of a relationship that meant so much for me for years was difficult, once I did, my entire world shifted. Soon I met like-minded people, other women who were practicing the Law of Attraction and on their own spiritual growth journey, soul sisters who would celebrate my success instead of trying to cut me down.

You may go through this same thing. You'll feel better than you have in a long time, and the people around you won't understand. Letting go of these relationships may hurt, but trying to hold on to them will hurt you the most. It will prevent you from being the person you are meant to be. It will be easier to let go of relationships that aren't allowing you to grow when you can trust the Universe is supporting you and it will bring you kinder, more loving, supportive people. The same thing can even happen with family members. When you become happier, they may make comments to try to bring you down. Their negative outlook on life is in direct conflict with your positive focus. Instead of expecting those people to come with you or see the world the way you do, just put your attention into your own growth. As you do this, you will attract more like-minded people. Ask your Universal helpers for more supportive friends and be open to the guidance you receive. You may feel inspired to join a new yoga studio, participate in a writers' group, go to a book launch party, attend a wellness meet-up, or take a solo trip to Europe. This is all part of your growth process.

It can sometimes be painful when people we care about don't grow with us, but sometimes people in our life aren't meant to go with us on our journey, so letting go is required for you to spread your wings.

Joy Jaunt: Allow Yourself to Grow

In order to allow ourselves to grow, we have to go inward to identify what is no longer working, needed, or flowing in our life.*

---

* This is inspired by Rebecca Campbell's Equinox Soul Inquiry.

Ask yourself these questions:

- What is becoming less important?
- How is life trying to change me? What is emerging?
- What old ways of being are no longer in alignment with who I am becoming?
- What is draining me and hard to hold on to?

Repeat the mantra, "I release what no longer serves me. All is in divine order."

Then repeat the mantra, "I am willing to live my life in new ways."

———

Today I am surrounded by women who I know would do anything for me, who support me and love me for who I am, and genuinely want to hear about my dreams and goals. Funny thing is, almost eight years later, that same friend I stopped taking to because she was negative about my focus and always picking on my positive outlook started to reach out. Today we are friends again, and would you believe she is now posting positive quotes on her social media pages and reading personal development books? She couldn't go on this journey until she was ready. For everyone there is a right path and the right time.

People come around in their own time. Everyone is on their own personal growth path and all you have to do is honor your own journey. Sometimes people ask, "Well what if it is a family member? I can't really escape people in my same household." If it is a family member who is negative, you get to choose to take on their fear or not. The more focused on feeling good you are, the easier it will be for you to be proud of your newfound peace. You won't take on others' energy because you are so comfortable with yourself. When family members or friends make negative comments, and try to make you feel bad for being you, simply recognize that it is not about you. Instead of taking on their negative energy, send them love and light. Remember everyone is on their own journey and you can be the light and inspiration to show them what is possible when you choose to be authentic. What others say about you says more about them than it does you. Remember that their comments really have nothing to do with you. When possible, don't be afraid to release relationships that are no longer working because you have friends waiting for you in other glorious places.

Radical Recap

As you grow, your friends will change. Let yourself shift and change and gravitate toward likeminded people.

AWESOME OPPORTUNITY: Find friends to support your new levels of joy and well-being.

MANTRA: "I surround myself with people who get, understand, and support me, and I do the same for them."

The Universal
Language

———

EMBRACE THE INSPIRATION
THAT COMES TO YOU

*And when you want something, all the Universe
conspires in helping you to achieve it.*
—Paulo Coelho

ONE OF THE BIGGEST REASONS we don't feel connected
to joy is because we don't trust ourselves or the inspiration that comes to us. As you begin to honor who you really
are, you will shift your awareness and you will get more insights and inspiration. Trusting this guidance and knowing
it is part of your happiness
will lead you forward with
more grace and ease.

Inspiration is the catalyst to your fulfillment.

———

Inspiration, in the form of
ideas that come to you, is the
Universe speaking to you.
The insights that come to you, come to you because they are
part of your own universal language with the source energy.

The universal language is your heart speaking to you. And when you have ideas and inspiration pop in your head, this is divinely inspired. When thinking about them brings you excitement, joy, and wonder, this is a signal that it is part of your path. Trusting this inspiration will lead you to fulfillment. We owe it to ourselves to honor these inspirations and trust them. So often we get inspired, but we doubt ourselves and don't know what step to take next. We become overwhelmed with the how: How much money will it take, how long will it take, how is it possible to go from where we are to what we really want to be? Doubt takes over and blocks us from moving forward.

By not taking action on our visions, we stay stuck. By ignoring our inner calling, we actually manifest the thing we don't want. We want clarity, but the clarity comes as we take action on these insights. Sometimes we think we don't know what we want, but we are getting clues through the visions that come to us, because they are the universal language of our heart. It's always talking to us. And our Universal helpers are always giving us clues. Almost everyone knows deep within themselves what they want, but so many of us answer this question with *I don't know*. When we say *I don't know what I want*, it is often because we are afraid. It is easier to say I don't know than to admit we are scared it won't work or that we feel unworthy of our desires, or we have no control over the manifestation. But every single person on earth has dreams, aspirations, and desires. It's a prerequisite to being human. But up until this point in our journey, most of us haven't allowed ourselves to dream bigger or at least go for what we really, truly want.

So it isn't so much that we don't know what we want, but we aren't listening or paying attention to our heart or the guidance. Our fear voice will try to tell us that we don't know what we want. The problem is that we actually believe the voice that tells us we don't know because we don't trust our heart.

Sometimes coaching clients come to me because they feel stuck, and they don't know what they want. I have found that, often, this not knowing had become their identity. I know when I was suffering from anxiety and depression, I had no idea what I wanted and this was something that actually became part of me, like the skin on my body. It was soothing to know I had no idea. It was something I clung to. Because as long as I said I didn't know what I wanted, I could stay stuck. And sometimes we choose to stay stuck because it is safer than admitting what we really want. Staying stuck is more manageable than the unknown, because sometimes admitting what we really want means exposing ourselves and being vulnerable. But I soon learned, as many of my coaching clients do, that not knowing what we want is often an excuse to keep us small. Instead of focusing on how you don't know, focus on asking the right questions. What is your greatest wish? What kind of life do you want to live?

It's not identifying what we want that scares us. It's realizing our life will change and we will have to face the unknown.

I believe we always know what we want, for when we drop into our heart, and ask our true self and our universal support system, we feel the truth within.

Think for a moment about what your greatest desire is. It's not to win the lottery or find your soul mate. It is deeper than that. I invite you to really uncover the core of your desires because this will be your path to connect to your true self.

Step 1: Identify what you want

Here are some common desires I hear in my coaching practice:

- Find my soul mate
- Explore the world
- Expand my social circle
- Be financially free
- Discover my purpose and passion
- Be healthy and fit

Step 2: Identify the essence/feeling

Now understand with each of these desires, there is a core feeling underneath that is driving this desire. Danielle Laporte talks about this in her book *The Desire Map: A Guide to Creating Goals with Soul*, and it is the foundation for the teaching of Esther and Abraham Hicks. Ask yourself what you truly want to feel. And then after you uncover that, you will understand your needs more deeply. Let's dissect them again.

- Find my soul mate—really means I want to feel loved for who I am
- Explore the world—really means I want to feel freedom
- Expand my social circle—I want to feel like I belong
- Be financially free—I want to feel secure
- Discover my purpose and passion—I want to feel a deeper sense of purpose and meaning
- Be healthy and fit—I want to feel self-love and be confident

Step 3: Give what you desire to yourself first

After you uncover your core feelings, you can let these drive you forward. This means if you've identified you want to feel secure, then you start practicing ways to feel more secure today. If you want to be loved for who you are, then you love yourself as you are right now. Give yourself what you want most, and soon your ideal life will just flow to you. There will no longer be this lack or focus on how stuck you feel.

Step 4: Recognize where energy is split

There is a misconception that when you focus on feeling good, it will come to you so much faster. This is sort of true, but if we have *split energy*, what we want will never come to us. As Esther Hicks teaches, split energy is your energy going in two different directions. Split energy is wanting it so badly but believing it can't happen. It is wanting it but being resentful when others have it. It is wanting it but doubting it is possible. It is wanting it but remembering how it hasn't happened for you in the past. Split energy blocks us from receiving what we truly desire. The way to overcome this is to recognize where your energy is split. By being aware, you can shift your focus to the desire and really practice feeling.

When my life coaching clients lack clarity, I ask them these questions, which always reveal their true desires.

1. If time, money, resources, energy weren't a factor, what would you want to do with your day?
2. What does your ideal life feel like?
3. If you knew you only had one year to live, what would you do?
4. What message does your future self have for you?

Ask yourself these same questions and you will soon see your deepest desire, your truth will be revealed. And any split energy you may have had will realign into one positive force forward. Once you identify what brings you joy, the only thing for you to do is commit to it. You do this by honoring it, massaging it, letting it join you every day. Trust your passion. You will begin to make it your purpose.

Some people push back here. They say, "Well I love drinking coffee, but I don't want to start my own coffee shop," or "I love to cook, but I don't want to be a chef," or "I love to sing, but it's way too difficult to break into the industry." This is missing the point. It is easy for us to want to quantify our passion. We immediately jump to all the reasons why it won't work, or how long it will take to build a business or dream, or how much money (that we don't currently have) it will take. Know that our ego naturally wants to know if it will work out so it will project the outcome before we even step on the path. But when we trust the universal language, the way of our heart, we can see it has nothing to do with the outcome, but everything to do with the joy. Expressing joy and feeling it fully is the outcome. Once we identify and commit to our passion, the fear will get louder.

Joy Jaunt: Become a Passionista with Purpose

Your fear will do everything it can to try to keep you safe, which means tricking you into thinking your passion is not a good idea to pursue. This looks like:

IDENTIFIED PASSION AND JOY: I love to travel

FEAR MIND TRICK 1: I don't have anyone to travel with, it is dangerous to travel alone, and I will get lonely.

FEAR MIND TRICK 2: You need a lot of money in order to do it, and you can't make money from traveling.

RESULT: No pins on the map, a dusty passport, and a bucket list left unchecked.

IDENTIFIED PASSION AND JOY: I love to paint and be creative.

FEAR MIND TRICK 1: You can't make a living doing what you love. Painting won't ever pay the bills.

FEAR MIND TRICK 2: What if no one will understand or like my painting style?

FEAR MIND TRICK 3: My second-grade teacher said I was not creative, and I should believe her because she clearly knows best.

RESULT: A whole bunch of canvases stuffed in your dark basement, an unsatisfied soul and sad heart.

IDENTIFIED PASSION AND JOY: I want to start dating again.

FEAR MIND TRICK 1: You've gained weight. You have to lose it all before you can start dating again.

FEAR MIND TRICK 2: I need time to date, and I am too busy with work right now. Besides I've been single for so long, I forgot how to actually flirt. Maybe it's changed since I last did it.

RESULT: Lonely days, sleepless nights and being consumed with worry.

After reviewing these examples, make your own list. What is your true joy? What are you passionate about? And what is the fear mind trick saying to try to keep you safe? Identifying them is the first path to removal.

Notice there may be multiple fear mind tricks. There are always many reasons your ego will come up with to try to prevent you from going after what you want. Because going after what you want is new, it is unpredictable, and the thing that scares your ego the most is not being in control. You can't control the outcome. Your ego truly thinks you could fail, but it is also concerned with your success. If you succeed and get what you want, then you won't need this fear, because you will be happy and fulfilled and connected to your authentic self. Also if you succeed and happiness is your outcome, then what will you do with that? You've spent most of your life not realizing your potential. You've spent years sad, frustrated, stuck in self-sabotaging habits; to break free from that is the scariest outcome because it represents freedom from fear. Up until this point in our journey, most of us have been relying on fear to get us through the day. We've leaned into it like comfort food, needing it to tell us things will not be okay so we can stay stuck in our anxiety. But we won't be letting fear rule the show anymore. And this is why the ego gets extra loud. As we become more aware of what we want, our ego/fear voice acts out. Be aware of how manipulative your fear mind is, but know that we always have a choice. We can start leaning into possibilities and believing in our future instead of leaning into our fear. The more guided action you take through fear, the more joyful your path will be.

Radical Recap

Get clear about what you want, because it is the key to your fulfillment.

AWESOME OPPORTUNITY: Trust your innermost desires and the inspiration that comes to you; take action on them.

MANTRA: "I follow through on the inspiration in my heart, I trust the process and let it flow."

The How Is in the Now

The next message you need is always right where you are.

—Ram Dass

WHAT IS THE FASTEST WAY to move through lack of clarity or fear? We take action! The best way to move through fear is to actually take steps toward your goals. With the vision in your heart, you know the dream you want realized. Ask yourself what one step you can take today. For the wanderluster, can you put a deposit down on the trip you keep dreaming about? For the painter, can you start a blog or Instagram account to share your art in a more public way? All you need to do is go inward and ask, "What is the

The more you trust your inner voice, the easier it becomes to follow through.

natural next action for me to take?" Your true self will reveal the right step. And one step at a time, one right action after another, you build your miraculous dream life.

When we take action, we are showing the Universe what we are moving toward is important to us. We matter and our dreams matter and the path becomes more clear. I always say the how is right now. The more steps you can take in the present, the more positive momentum you will create toward your ideal life. Focus forward with clarity and take more guided action. The key word being *guided*.

> **The fastest way to manifest your desires is to take guided action daily.**

Taking action blindly will reap poor results. If you are hustling and trying hard to make it happen without focusing on your energy, you will be exhausted, frustrated, and even become resentful. The golden rule for manifesting what you want is to focus on your vibration. As you focus on how you want to feel, you will get more guidance because you are a clear channel connecting to your true self. Inspired action can come to us in our dreams, in conversations, in meditation, and in prayers. Once you identify your desire, the Universe will send you messengers—people, ideas, and concepts that can help you move forward. Our job is to pay attention to these messengers. When I decided to take my trip, I started meeting more travelers. I would see more books, ideas, and TV shows on the destinations I was going to go. Inspiration was everywhere, because I was clear within myself about what I wanted.

The Universe is always speaking to you. It will send you little messages. You may think it is a coincidence, but everything is part of your universal plan and the desires you've put forth. So look around and believe in something more, because that something more is guiding you. It is your helper in achieving all that you desire.

When you are clear about what you want, the Universe will swoop in to support you and give you what you need.

Even with these signs and daily nudges, we still want to know the *how*. How will it happen? When will it happen? How do I get from here to there? How can I feel more balanced and joyful? HOW??? I will be honest with you: The how doesn't matter. There is no one way to do anything. Your how is totally different from someone else's how. There is no direct path. It is all part of your own journey. That's why in my author mentorship program I never tell an author exactly how to get a book agent or land a book deal, but rather how to trust the guidance coming to them so they can honor their own path with the Universe. Of course I share industry standard practices, but I know that we all have our own how. For example, one client met her agent at a writers' conference, whereas another pitched multiple agents and after a year of rejections, landed her dream publishing deal without an agent. Another client landed her dream book deal after a television appearance on a national talk show, and still another's self-published book got picked up by a mainstream publisher. Same result—the desire to have a book deal—but all different ways. The how is not as important as we make it in our minds. It is the Universe's job to do your how. So I would be doing you a huge disservice by telling you how, because there is no one how. And that is what this entire book is about: honoring your own path and discovering your soul's unique language. You can learn the tools and I can show you ideas, but the exact how is between you and your true self. The how is already inside of you with the guidance you are constantly receiving. So it comes down to trusting and believing in yourself. When we align with our true self we can never go wrong.

The steps we take now are the how, but they must be inspired by our inner guide for true success. There are life lessons you need to learn, and your how will be of the highest good for your own soul's growth. And often it looks nothing like anyone else's. So many people get overwhelmed when they think about moving forward because they feel they lack the clarity. They focus on the how, and what steps they *should* take to move forward on their dream, but this "needing to know the how" is another sneaky ego trick. And it's keeping you playing small. So instead of asking how, get busy focusing on inspired action now. Of course we can get inspiration from others, but it's important to honor your own path by knowing the how is in the guidance you are receiving now.

Furthermore, the how is not really anything we need to concern ourselves with because the how is the Universe's job. In Rhonda Byrne's book *The Secret*, she talks about the how. "*How it will happen, how the Universe will bring it to you, is not your concern or your job. Allow the Universe to do it for you. When you're trying to work out HOW it will happen, you are emitting a frequency that contains lack of faith—that you don't believe you have it already. You think you have to do it and you do not believe the Universe will do it for you. The how is not your part in the creative process.*"

So simply relax into your life just a little bit more, and instead of needing to know the how, trust the now.

Radical Recap

To overcome lack of clarity take action. The more you move forward, the more the path reveals itself.

AWESOME OPPORTUNITY: Focus on what you can do right now to move yourself forward.

MANTRA: "The how is in the now. I embrace the moment and make the most out of it."

Go on a
Future Field Trip

EMBRACE YOUR IDEAL LIFE

*What you want is already here, in the unified
field of pure potential. Everything you need to
fulfill your greatest desire is already part of your
being. But it can't come out until you align with
it, let go of the obstructions to it, and raise your
vibration to the level at which it already exists.*
                              —DEREK RYDALL

*I*F YOU CAN THINK IT and you believe it, it is a possible
outcome for you. In quantum physics and from a spiritual perspective, what you want already exists. Knowing this
can help us feel more secure in our process of manifesting
our ideal life, but the frustration comes when we are clear
but we begin to doubt ourselves. That's why it's important to
get clear about what you want and tap into your own inner
potential. Many of us focus on what is, and we don't always
like it so we stay stuck in the current situation. But there is

a powerful law of the Universe that can actually help you get unstuck. I call it *future field trip.*

Start to think more about what might be. Take time to go to your heart and ask what does my ideal life really feel like? What do I want for my time here on earth? It is perfectly okay to spend some time hoping, wishing, and dreaming. Treat this visualization process like a daily exercise and as you practice it, it will become easier. Thinking about new possibilities is an important part of the manifestation process, because it will open new doors and realities for you and loved ones. The future field trip is where you visualize yourself living your ideal life. For many months I did this. I imagined myself traveling the world because I love to explore and see new places. I pictured myself having the freedom to write books from anywhere and reach people's hearts with my examples and stories. I saw myself on stages all around the world, inspiring people to believe and trust themselves. It was in my mind first. I believed it and today I am it—this is my current life. I created it first by visualizing and believing in it daily.

As we honor our curiosity we start to see our truth, which is what brings us joy is always worth pursuing.

Joy Jaunt: Future Field Trip

Spend three to five minutes every day visualizing the type of life you want to live. Imagine the people, places, feelings, and experiences associated with this type of lifestyle. Visualize it, feel it, practice it in your mind. As you do this, you will start to feel more faith build within you and your confidence will increase. Have fun in your mind first, and soon you will see it manifested in your life.

Don't shy away from these insights. Go on future field trips as often as you can. The more you can see it, the more you will believe it and feel it. Visualizing yourself and life the way you want it to be is part of connecting to your joy. Take time each day to visualize yourself living your ideal life. Even if what you are experiencing right now seems so different from what you want, keep focusing on what you want. The ideas wouldn't come to you if they weren't possible for you. Align with your vision and let this lead you forward.

> *Your imagination is a powerful tool. The insights, visions, and ideas that come to you are part of your fulfillment.*

Radical Recap

If you can think about it, it is possible for you. Your ideal life is your future self showing you what's possible.

AWESOME OPPORTUNITY: Picture yourself doing what you want, with whom you want, when you want.

Your ideal life starts right now, with you being able to imagine it.

MANTRA: "What brings me joy is always worth pursuing."

Joy Seeker Journal Time

In your workbook or joy journal, take a moment to answer these questions before progressing to the next section.

- If time, money, resources, energy weren't a factor, what would I want to do with my life?
- What am I learning on the way to reaching my desires?
- What insights have I been receiving from my Universal support?
- What message does my future self have for me?

Self-expression

IS THE
HIGHEST
FORM OF
HAPPINESS

#JoySeeker

PART 4

THE ACCEPTING

How to Be Who You Are Meant to Be in a World That Tells You You Should Be Different

Honor Your Own Poetry Within

ACCEPT YOUR UNIQUE TALENTS AND PASSION

If you can't figure out your purpose, figure out your passion. For your passion will lead you right into your purpose.

—BISHOP T.D. JAKES

WHEN IS THE LAST TIME you looked at someone and thought they had it so much better than you? That if only you had what they had, you would be able to feel more joy? Welcome to the biggest barrier to our joy: comparison. We often look outside of ourselves at what everyone else is doing, and of course they seem so happy and more put together, which often makes us feel even more off track and behind in life.

Comparing myself to others blocked me from feeling joy for the first few years of my career as a writer. I would always compare myself to other authors who were further along in their careers. There was one author in particular, who was actually a friend and mentor, whom I was insanely jealous of. Every book she released became an instant *New York Times* bestseller, her book tours where sold out across the world, and her courses were always filled to capacity with a waiting list a mile long. It was as if the abundance gods had blessed her with the Midas touch. Everything she created and released was gold; even Oprah approved. Needless to say, when I compared myself to her, I always felt I couldn't ever measure up and I worried that I would never be good enough.

For a little while, I actually became so focused on her career, trying to dissect the formula for success. I was determined to figure out what she was doing that I wasn't. For starters, she probably wasn't consumed with worry about what others were doing. She probably didn't compare herself to others, either. She was busy creating content she loved and being in her joy. If I was focusing on others, it would keep me from accessing my own joy. It occurred to me that joy is the path to success. As long as I was worried about what people thought of me, or worried about what other people were doing, I was not present in my own creation process. When we compare ourselves to others, we stay outside of our own potential. We wonder, *Why do they have what I don't? Why are they so lucky? How can I get what they have?* But really what we seek is not what they have, because everyone is on their own path, but we like what they represent. What we see in them is joy, happiness, peace, connection, and we want to experience that, too. When we see someone who has what we want, they are connected to their joy. What we see is their joy and that is what we want most. Which often makes us feel even more disconnected from our true selves.

We all also want acknowledgment and approval. We care deeply about other people's approval, and this in itself can

prevent us from moving forward. When we need the approval of others, our actions
and even our lack of actions
are based on something outside of ourselves. We want

When we look outside of ourselves, we believe what we are not.

others to approve of us, so we make choices based on others,
not choices inspired by our true self.

For many years I wanted other authors who were further
along in their careers to approve, acknowledge, and support
my work. I saw it as a stamp of validation that I was worthy
to play in the same arena. Looking back, I see how insanely
silly this is, but this is what our mind will do. The ego will convince us that what we believe is true. I believed some
big-name author supporting my work meant I was a good
writer. But really the two have nothing to do with each other.
Thinking like this, my worth was based solely on someone
else's approval. It had nothing to do with what I did or what I
actually accomplished. None of that mattered; it was all about
what someone else thought. I gave away my power and was
waiting for someone else to give me value. That was crazy! I
was creating false idols and letting them determine my worth.

A false idol is something or someone we admire and idolize that actually keeps us from seeing and expressing our own
true light. I'm not saying we can't admire and respect people.
It's a great idea to recognize success and have role models we
can look to for inspiration. But we shouldn't let anyone else
decide who we are, who we should be, and if we are worthy.
We have to look at our projections and false idols and say,
"You know what? I don't believe you are better than me; we
are all equals. You are no longer something I will give my
attention to." When we release the energetic focus we have

on others, we can return to ourselves. We have to remember our true power lies within ourselves. It is the light within our own self, the love that is our most authentic power. As long as we are focusing on others, we will never feel good enough. Whether it's a coworker, a family member, or celebrity, you give your power away when you think others are better than you. We convince ourselves that our happy will come when we get more recognition, success, and money, like the people we admire. We work endless hours, then identify with our exhaustion and stress like a badge of honor.

One thing that's been refreshing while traveling is the relaxed European approach to life. Many cultures in Europe put family first; in some countries they take siestas, they spend hours in the cafés or parks socializing, and they allow themselves to just be instead of always rushing to do one thing or another. In adopting this way of life, I feel more balanced and at peace. I no longer focus on others, and instead appreciate myself and my own journey. Too many of us don't know how to be present or relax. This is in part because we've placed our focus on the wrong things. We think joy will come from something outside of us, in something we do or achieve, but in our heart we know this is not true. This is the disconnect and why we feel like something is off. It's time to bring your attention back to you.

Joy Jaunt: Become Your Own Hero

So often we look outside of ourselves at others and want what they have, but as long as we do this, we prevent ourselves from truly seeing our own beautiful light. Identify a famous person, a public personality, or someone you deeply admire Ask yourself what it is you like about them. Maybe you like their carefree attitude or their fun-loving personality. Maybe they are living the type of lifestyle you aspire to, or maybe they are getting the success and rewards you seek. Then remind yourself you don't truly know anything about them or what is going on in their life, so take your focus off them and recognize the things you like about this person are also within you. You can still appreciate and love them, but love yourself first. Maybe you want to be more carefree and fun loving. Cultivate ways you can do this in your own day-to-day life and let yourself shine your own wonderful light. Now you can take your attention off others so you can show up more fully for yourself. When we do this, we get our own power back and feel more aligned with our beautiful bright self.

⸻

Still it's easier said than done. When we compare ourselves to others, sometimes we imitate them without even realizing it. I recall in my first year teaching and leading courses, I saw a lecture title that my life coach used and it was widely successful. So I used the same language and called my online workshop a similar title. Well you can guess what happened. For her: She had a sold-out crowd. It later turned into a book that became a *New York Times* bestseller and she even was featured on Oprah talking about the ideas. But for me, a handful of people signed up and it fizzled fast, both the enthusiasm and the support. I learned quickly that what works for others will not necessarily work for me because the truth is, every single person is on their own path. I recognized that my own path looks nothing like anyone else's, and today my life looks much different. I no longer look outside of myself for approval or recognition, and I am clear about who I am and what my message is. Looking back, I can see that I didn't really want to teach on that topic. I just saw that it worked for her, so I thought, surely, if it worked for her, it will work for me.

If we aren't connected to our self, we will misdirect our energy and give away our power.

So many of us blindly imitate others without even realizing it. We do this when we are unsure of ourselves. But trying to mimic others will never give you the real, authentic connection to your true self that you want. When we mimic or look to others to help us solve our own problems we are doing ourselves a disservice, because our answers aren't out there. They are inside of us. Sure we can look to others to see what they are doing and gain inspiration. Like my mentor, I'd still like to be endorsed by Oprah and be on national television. I still want a number one multiweek *New York Times* bestselling book. But she has her own path, and I have mine. I plan to reach this outcome in my own unique way, a way that aligns with my true self. Glennon Doyle said, "We're only envious of those already doing what we are made to do. Envy is a giant flashing arrow pointing us toward our destiny." The turning point for me was when I started to look at the people I was jealous of and seeing they were showing me what is possible. I replaced my jealousy with appreciation by honoring them on their path. I energetically thanked them for being a light to shine on my path forward.

As you move through the stages of your own journey, you will soon learn that there is no competition at all because you are your own being on your own unique journey. The more we compare and compete with others, the longer we stray from our own plan. I asked myself, "What is most important to me? What brings me the most joy?" It just so happens traveling and writing and sharing my experience with others is my fulfillment. Growing spiritually and emotionally is fulfillment to me, and being able to express my true self in a world that tells me to do otherwise is the ultimate form of fulfillment. So here I am living it. As I travel the world I feel connected to my best self. I tried to imagine the people I used to compare myself to doing the same thing as me, traveling full-time as a travel writer, life coach, speaker, and self-explorer, and I couldn't. It isn't part of their path or plan. My life feels like my destiny, and that is when you know you are being true to yourself. When it feels like you can't *not* do it, because you feel so alive when you are living your truth. The magic of Joy Seeking is, you honor your own path. Be true to you.

So how do you stop comparing yourself to others? You discover and honor the poetry within you. What is the poetry? It is your passion.

To understand the true you, tap into your own poetry; discover the thing that makes you feel alive. What makes

Passion is pure energy, and the more you honor it, the more you will live a life that excites you.

you feel alive and connected to you? What joyful activity do you turn to when things get hard? The more you do it, the more connected to you you feel. And when you honor this path, you honor your true self, and there is no comparison. When we stop comparing ourselves to others or needing their approval, and focus on appreciating and approving ourselves, everything starts to fall into place. For me, my passion is writing. But back when I was in a corporate career, I didn't know this was my passion. But the clues were there. I was always writing—in my journal, on the back of napkins. It was how I best knew how to express myself and I loved it. It brought me immense joy. It was my poetry. Soon my stories were getting published and the path showed me that my passion could be a fulfilling career. I didn't have to force anything. I allowed it to flow. Let your passion flow.

In the book *Big Magic, Creative Living Beyond Fear*, Elizabeth Gilbert talks about the early stages of her writing career. She never put pressure on her craft to make money. She knew she wanted to be a professional writer, but in the beginning she took all kinds of odd jobs to pay the bills. She wasn't trying to become famous or write books that would reach over twenty million people. She just knew she needed to write. It was her own form of poetry.

The passion within you, first and foremost, is *for* you. The by-product of you honoring your own passion is being able to share it with others. The one thing the world's most successful people have in common is they honor their poetry, the passion within. They set out to do what they loved, and most didn't even think about becoming famous, rich, or successful from their passion. They just

> *Honor what moves you. Trust it. Dive into it and let it become your way of life.*

knew they needed to honor their passion, because like poetry, it moved them.

The more you trust your own journey, the more you will see that there is no real comparison, because you are honoring your own path. Once we understand that every single person on earth has his or her own path and poetry, and it looks nothing like anyone else's, then freedom prevails. You will get to a place where you no longer compare, but you celebrate others on their own journey. Now I salute my coach and author friends. The people who used to trigger me, I now celebrate and support fully. Because I honor them on their journey and know that I am in mine. I no longer get jealous because I no longer question their success or compare my journey to theirs. Now when I see them hit bestseller lists or reach new career heights, I enthusiastically cheer for them, because one person showing up fully and living their potential is power to all of us.

To send negative thoughts, resentments, anger, or jealousy to another is not only spreading negativity, but it is

When one person wins, we all win.

harming you. Instead, we can focus on lifting each other up by celebrating one another. When others are doing well, we can honor them on their path with love and gratitude.

Some of us have a belief that there is not enough to go around, and when another person is winning, that means less of the success pie for us. However, this is just another story blocking us, a fear trick keeping us small. Not having enough is an illusion. We live in an abundant Universe, where we can manifest whatever we want. Step into your own power by feeling joy for others. Much of our own

The Universe is an abundant playground of opportunities, and what is meant for you will never pass you by.

happiness comes from supporting others. And there is plenty of success and joy to go around.

Instead of focusing on others, focus on yourself and your own path. You are enough and that is all you need to do to move forward and be fulfilled.

Radical Recap

Looking outside of yourself for approval or comparing yourself to others will never give you the peace you need.

AWESOME OPPORTUNITY: Recognize your true power is within you. You are on your own unique path and what works for you is different from what works for everyone else. Take more steps to honor your passion and follow through on your curiosity.

MANTRA: "I honor my own path."

Don't Shy away from Your Authentic Shine

ACCEPT YOUR LIGHT

*People who want the most approval get the least
and the people who need approval the least get
the most.*

—Wayne Dyer

You have tendencies that are natural to you. No one else in the world is you, and that is your special, unique path. When you stop comparing yourself to others, you will be free to tap into your inner sense of wonder. This is your unique point of view, your natural habits, which I call your authentic shine. It's your light. When you can see how magnificent you truly are, self-actualization and realization present themselves fully. When you begin to trust and believe in yourself, you step into a new sense of understanding yourself and your place in the world. You no longer take things so seriously or personally, because you are immersing yourself in the play and joy of being alive. Most importantly, when you trust yourself and shine your light, you have self-confidence that is undeniable, and this is when you become unapologetic about who you are and what you stand for. Soon you will see that your life unfolds in ways that are miraculous.

But how do we learn to believe and trust in ourselves? The answer is simple: We fully commit to being ourselves. In showing up more fully, we build trust with ourselves. We begin to see that showing those weird habits, or saying what we really want to say, isn't as scary or bad as our fear made it out to be. The more you show of yourself, the easier it is for others to understand, support and love you.

Although I didn't know it at the time, when I set out to travel the world I was looking outside of myself for what I needed to discover within. I was seeking fulfillment and joy in places, in new experiences, and the people I met, but this is an extraordinary amount of pressure to put on one thing. As I dived fully into my journey, I learned that the real joy is not outside of me. It is only to be found within. Joy was with me always, I just had to allow it. Once I discovered this, I realized I can be anywhere in the world and have this feeling. Joy isn't outside of us in the next thing we do or the place we go. It is who we are at our core.

To be authentic and connect with our true self, we must stop shining light on things we are not.

We spend years, decades, lifetimes chasing this peace, but it is never outside of us. When you let yourself be more of who you really are, you see that peace is part of your own pulse. I discovered this when I was traveling the world, alone on my solo trip. Traveling alone brought great clarity that what I do and where I go has nothing to do with

my worth or fulfillment. Life is about joy, and when you realize *you* are the joy, you start to reframe your life in a way that
supports that fully.

The greatness we are all seeking isn't outside of ourselves.
It isn't in the next big adventure, or achievement, or bucket
list item we check off. We bring our greatness from within.
It is us as we are right now. Here and now, we are enough.

Once you understand that you are enough, you will feel so
connected, peaceful, and aligned. The presence of love is within
you and you are embraced by all of the divine source energy.
You are one with the Universe. But how do we get there? How
do we truly know that we are enough? By not shying away
from our authentic shine. Your authentic shine is you in your
entirety. It is your essence, all of you in your wonderful glory.
So many of us have pieces of us we hide away. If only that part
of me wasn't here, then I would be happier. That double chin,
the cellulite, the way we talk, or mispronounce words, our
frizzy hair or freckled face. However, the thing about you that
you dislike is part of your authentic shine because it is part of
you. We tend to let our insecurities define us, and when we do
this we can't connect to joy.
But we also have things about
ourselves that are pretty cool,
and we hide those things as
well. Maybe you are really
talented at something, but
when someone else compli-
ments you on it, you deflect or

> *"You playing small does
> not serve anyone."*
> *—Marianne
> Williamson*

quickly change the subject. Pushing away your greatness and
deflecting is a tactic our ego does to keep us trapped in insecurity and self-doubt. We worry so much about looking conceited
or egotistical that we ignore the good aspects of ourselves.

Your true self knows that you are amazing, so when you deflect compliments or push away your good qualities, this hurts the real you. You weaken your connection to yourself, and your ego loves this, because the weaker and more insecure you are, the easier it is to manipulate and control you. The fix is to see that it is more than okay to see and show how amazing you are.

For decades I was running from myself because I didn't believe I was worth it. I felt unlovable and didn't acknowledge the light within me. I focused more on my flaws and insecurities. But when I found self-love, I discovered that most of us are not afraid of our dark, but actually the light within us. We are terrified of being great; we don't want to outshine those around us. Society, history, and culture prove if you show too much light, then you are different, therefore misunderstood, intimidating, someone to be feared. But dimming our light is a disservice to ourselves and to the world. We are all made for greatness, we all have a purpose. Allow your light to shine! Celebrating you is not egotistical or selfish. It is an act of self-love.

You don't have to change yourself to love yourself. You just have to be more of yourself.

⏤

If you avoid acknowledging your amazingness, you'll never feel the true connection to your gorgeous self. Your true self is awesome, beautiful, super abundant, grateful, and secure. And there is a nothing wrong with seeing how wonderful you truly are. It is time to celebrate and honor the true you.

Some of us deflect compliments or hide a piece of us to try to fit in. We lessen our shine to collectively squeeze into the crowd. But this hurts us even more.

While I was traveling I met a lot of people who were on vacation. We would meet up for dinner or meet for coffee, and many of the people I met would react negatively when I told them I was a full-time traveler. I would instantly feel their jealousy and see their body language shift. Some would even make comments. One woman called me a bitch, then tried to laugh it off as if she was joking, but I could feel her resentment. I was doing what so many people could only dream of doing. I was living my dream fully. The negativity I received shocked me because here I was following my heart and being true to myself. I thought, *Isn't that what we all want for each other?* After a few months of constantly feeling bad after I told people I was a full-time traveler, I decided to shy away from my truth and just downplay my lifestyle. It seemed a lot easier than trying to deal with more criticism, or so I thought. When I next met a couple who asked me what I did for a living, instead of telling them I was a full-time traveler, I simply said I was a writer on vacation. As we continued our conversation, the couple told me they were full-time travelers, digital nomads from the Netherlands. They, too, could work from anywhere and were working from all over Europe for the summer. I laughed to myself because the first time I decided to shy away from expressing my full truth and downplaying my awesomeness, the Universe brought me a couple who did exactly what I did. I knew then that I don't need to hide myself or shy away from my greatness. If others can't handle your brightness, that is not your issue. It is more about them and their own path than it is yours. Keep shining your gorgeous light because the world needs you as you are.

You should never ever hide your true self or downplay who you are to make others comfortable. If someone else is uncomfortable with you, your lifestyle choices, or point of view, that's because your amazingness brings up something within them that they haven't looked at. When you commit to the light and live a life that feels good and is aligned with who you really are, this can be intimidating for those who are not living as fully or authentically as you are. Being great is a birthright for all of us, but only some choose to step into their light. You have arrived at the place in your life where you will no longer hide or hold back your true self from anyone. If it makes others uncomfortable, that shouldn't take you out of your own joy. What you can do is send others love and light and a mini prayer that they find the happiness and connection to self that you have discovered.

There is nothing wrong with you being who you are meant to be, and the more you honor your true self, the more freedom and inner peace you will feel.

The more true to yourself you are, the more jealous people may be because you are doing what so many are scared to do. You are living an authentic life. But this way of life, being true to yourself, is freedom, and you shouldn't give up that freedom for anything else in the world, especially not to make others more comfortable. Sacrificing your happiness to make others comfortable serves no one. Your focus is to be true to you, for this is the highest form of happiness.

Joy Jaunt: Free-Write Your Way to Freedom

Ask yourself the following questions:

Is there someone in my life I am uncomfortable showing the real me?
Where have I been downplaying my awesomeness?
How is this affecting my well-being?
What do I sacrifice in order to make others happy?
What is hiding my true self costing me?

Make a vow to be more of you in all areas of your life, including around the people who make you uncomfortable.

When you hold back who you really are to please others, the person you hurt the most is yourself. We have to be 100 percent true to ourselves and this includes owning up to your awesomeness. Yes, you are awesome!

Radical Recap

You don't need to be afraid to be yourself. The world needs you to show more of your true self. You will feel freedom and peace when you express yourself fully. You are light and love. Shine brightly.

AWESOME OPPORTUNITY: Don't let others try to bring you down. Keep shinning your light and be an example for others of what's possible when you believe and trust yourself.

MANTRA: "I am unapologetic about showing my true self. I am light and love and I express it fully."

Selfish Sanity

ACCEPT YOUR NEEDS

*Self-care is never a selfish act—it is simply good
stewardship of the only gift I have, the gift I was
put on earth to offer to others.*

—Parker Palmer

So many of us are reluctant to go after what we want because we think following our dreams and doing what we truly want is selfish. I see this in many of my coaching clients. They tell me, "Who am I to go after what I want?" Who are they not to?

But I actually understand them; I used to think things like "Who wants to read anything I have to say; who am I to write about my personal experience and share insights with others?" This self-deprecation has been handed down to us from our parents and their parents before; it is ingrained in certain cultures. And it becomes a part of us. If you break away to follow your heart, you will be deemed selfish. How dare you go

195

after what you really want? Who are you to follow your heart? I will always remember the very last day of my advertising job. I pulled coworkers aside and told them I was resigning, and the look on their face said it all. There was worry, fear, and shock mixed with extreme jealousy and confusion. I was doing what so many of us feel in our hearts but are terrified to do: I was being true to myself. I was honoring my heart's pull and living in alignment with me. I could see them thinking: *How dare you, who are you, what makes you so special?* But the truth is we all are this special. We all have this power to align with who we really are. It just takes a willingness to step away from the crowd and trust the rhythm of your own heart.

Choosing to do things for you and following your heart is the ultimate act of self-love and self-care.

What often gets overlooked in the wellness community is what happens after you start being true to yourself. When you are aligned with your authentic self, you will sometimes have what looks like massive redirects. Change in course; new life plans; leaving jobs, relationships, places; and even old dreams will no longer feel good. This is life asking you to grow more into your true self. But change has to happen. The more honest you become with yourself and the more layers you peel back, the more truth you will reveal. And this may look like a major upset in your life. But that's only if you are clinging to the old, trying to hold on to something you have outgrown. If you follow your heart and stay true to yourself, beautiful things will happen.

How do you follow your heart and be true to yourself? You listen to and understand your feelings. Your feelings are a direct path to your joy. You are now living at a level where you are more connected to yourself, more aligned with who you really are and what you need to be happy. When you are true to yourself, you learn that it is okay to change your mind. That is what real growth is: aligning with your heart in each and every moment of your life. At one point in your life, your heart may crave freedom, travel, and exploration (like mine did), and you follow through and give yourself what you need. Later, you may go inward and listen carefully to learn what you crave now is structure, routine, family, and connection. That's okay. We change and our desires change. So many of us put so much pressure on our choices. We think the choices we make are supposed to be our end-all decision, but life is about exploration, creative urges, and diving more fully into who you really are. Follow-through is not as important as listening to our heart. And true happiness is when we make all choices aligned from our heart. Your heart is your truth, it knows you, and when you listen to it and follow through on the guidance, it will show you the way to fulfillment and inner peace.

The safest place in the world to be yourself is within your heart.

I spent decades afraid of what people would think if I showed the real me. I was terrified of being made fun of, or worse, not being accepted. A personality trait of mine is to see things as positive and loving; I am a glass half-full girl and an eternal optimist. I have the ability to make any situation seem better by climbing my thoughts into a happier state. Which suits me well as a personal development author and inspirational speaker, but growing up I was made fun of for being a positive girl. In third grade the song by Bobby

McFerrin "Don't Worry Be Happy" came out and I instantly fell in love. The song was catchy and fun, and I popped it in my Walkman, and danced around the playground. Well, other kids didn't love the song so much, and the repetition drove them crazy. They complained to the teachers that I was too happy and it was annoying. (Yes, this happened when I was nine years old. Children were complaining about my positivity, so I got pretty used to not fitting in because of this natural trait of mine.) The teachers told me that I couldn't play the song anymore and took my music away. I felt mortified, sad, and extremely confused. I was just happy and doing something that was natural to me—singing and dancing—and because the rest of the kids didn't like it, I was being punished. My ego took over and fear and pain tried to protect me, teaching me that I would never be accepted for who I truly am so I should hide my true self. That's when the first of my eating disorders started. At age nine I began to binge eat, trying to stuff my feelings of not fitting in and feeling unlovable. Once I entered high school, my overeating turned into not eating, and I suffered silently from more disorders. But it wasn't the disorders that were the real problem. They were a Band-Aid over the deeper issue: that I was hiding the real me from the world. I hated my body, I hated myself. But how could I love myself if I wasn't even giving myself the chance to be myself? Interestingly enough, the eating disorders disappeared when I found self-love and embraced the true me. By showing up more fully in the world as me, I healed my emotional pain, I stopped caring so much about what others thought, and I realized how exhausting it was to try to pretend, to hide, to force anything that wasn't real. So I dropped the entire pretense and started to reveal more of the real me. Having an "I don't need others' approval because

I approve of myself" attitude is freeing. There is great joy in not worrying about what others think of you. Of course I am still human and it hurts when people don't accept me or leave a bad review, comment, or say something rude, but I've learned to detach, not take it so personally, let it roll off my back more easily. Adopting the mentality that you don't need others' approval will be one of the fastest ways for you to reclaim joy.

Connecting with others is important for us and we crave acceptance. So as an adult, I started to build positive communities on the web, places where people who felt the way I did could have a place to feel seen and heard. I did this online, via social media and with my weekly blog, playwiththeworld .com. The more me I started to show, the more balanced and rewarding my life was. I spent decades trying to hide myself from the world, because I thought the world wouldn't accept me. After all, past experience proved that. But the more I gave myself permission to show up and shine my real light, the happier, healthier, and more peaceful my life became. Today, I don't shy away from my true self and I don't care too much about others' opinions of me, because I know it shows more about them and who they are than it does me. I got to a point where I realized life is short. We don't know how much time we have, and if we are spending our life living for others, or hiding ourselves to try to fit in, then we are wasting our precious time.

Plus, the most amazing thing happens when you start to show the world the real you: Not only are your needs now being met, you get an honest reflection back. The world can finally see you in all your glory and will in turn love back at you. The wrong people we spent so many years trying to fit in with and be accepted by will fall away and your true tribe will show up. The people who get you, who want you in their life and need you, will emerge.

You must be true to yourself in order to attract more kind, loving people into your life. As you recall, the number one regret people have on their death bed is, *I wish I had lived a life true to myself instead of the life others had wanted for me.* So many of us live for others. We put them first because we don't acknowledge our own greatness, because we shy away from our own light. But when we do this we are depleted, sad, and always feel like something is off. Not to mention it is painful to be someone you are not. Your capacity to feel joy is directly related to how much you care about yourself. Practice self-love and don't be afraid to be who you really are.

> **Your true tribe can't show up until you do.**

Radical Recap

It just takes a willingness to step away from the crowd and trust the rhythm of your own heart, but it is worth it because you will finally feel peace, acceptance, and joy. The more you give yourself permission to show up and shine your real light, the happier, healthier, and more peaceful you'll be.

AWESOME OPPORTUNITY: Get to know the real you and express yourself more often.

MANTRA: "I don't need others' approval because I approve of myself."

I'd Rather Be Me

ACCEPT YOURSELF

To love oneself is the beginning of a life-long romance.

—OSCAR WILDE

*Y*OU WILL GET TO A place in your journey where it will be so exhausting to be anything less than who you really are. Many of us are used to hiding parts of ourselves and not being true to ourselves, but the more you commit to joy and self-love, the harder it will be to hide your shine. Other people may not understand your brightness, and this is because they are still consumed in their own journey. But you just keep being you, because you have the opportunity to shine more light into the world.

The more you are connected to your light, the easier it will be to navigate your life. How do we connect with our light? We practice it daily. What does your well-being practice look like? When I was at a wellness retreat in Costa Rica,

The world does not benefit from you playing small. Your light is what heals; your light is what the world needs.

one of the instructors spoke about the power of a spiritual practice. He asked, "How many of you have a spiritual practice?" I looked around the room and I was one of the only people who didn't raise my hand. I thought to myself, *I don't have a regular practice; I am the practice.* My life feels good. I am balanced, happy, and living my ideal life. I don't have to practice what I am. This was a radical new concept for me because for so many years I looked at health, well-being, and my own self-love as something I had to try to be conscious of and make a habit. But you will arrive to a place where your dedicated focus results in a new normal, and that normal feels good. You adjust to a life without struggle, without drama. You are living your new peaceful normal. Welcome to the real you. The real goal is to be you and participate in the things that make you feel like your best self. Sometimes when we think of practice we think of work, but self-care is joyful, it is fun. When I have a good spin bike workout, spend the day at the beach, or have a solid writing session, I feel aligned with my best self. What brings you closer to your best self? Do these activities daily.

Joy Jaunt: Me Matters Time

First identify what you enjoy doing. Make a list of the times you feel you are your best self. What are you doing?

Who are you with? Do you enjoy spending time in nature, creating art, philosophical conversations? Set aside time to do what you love. Call this *me matters time*. You will feel better when you give yourself the love and care you so often give out to others. Set aside time each day to do what makes you feel like your best self.

Radical Recap

Self-Love is the highest form of happiness. When you show up for yourself daily and commit to your joy it becomes a regular way of life.

AWESOME OPPORTUNITY: Stop trying so hard to be healthy and happy, and let your practice be your lifestyle.

MANTRA: "When I take care of myself, I can show up more fully in the world. My well-being is priority."

Sharing Is Caring

—

ACCEPT YOUR PAST

*To get the full value of joy you must have some-
one to divide it with.*

—MARK TWAIN

HAVE YOU EVER NOTICED THAT people who seem happiest and healthiest are also very loving and caring?
They give their time, money, or energy to causes they care
about or to friends and family who need help. When we show
up fully for ourselves, our love cup will be full to the brim; we
will want to share this love with the world. Once I found happiness past my depression, I wanted to share it. I felt that I
had arrived at a place of understanding and healed myself. I
shared what I learned on my blog, and in this way I was then
able to pass on these lessons and help others. Sharing our
journey openly with others *is* part of our own healing quest.

You may get to a point where you've arrived. You feel happier and healthier and you feel an inner desire to help others

by sharing your truth undefined. Whether it is writing a book, speaking more about what you've been through, giving your time, starting a charity, investing your own time into more philanthropic activities, or helping and supporting others, giving of yourself is the true value of your life. Many of us go through difficult times and experience heartbreaking situations, and we overcome them. When we do, we feel empowered from within and feel compelled to share and pass on the inner knowing that comes with our own resiliency. You genuinely want to help and serve others.

You have gifts, talents, skills that you have mastered, and sharing them is part of the cycle of fulfillment.

A beautiful example of this idea is demonstrated by my mentor and dear friend Summer Bacon. Growing up, she was extremely shy and didn't have a lot of close friends. She's been through some incredibly difficult experiences in life, including surviving rape and an abusive marriage. For many years, she suffered silently with depression and struggled with being on earth. But she loves to write and decided to write a book detailing some of her life experiences. She discovered in writing her own story not only was she able to heal more of herself, but she could also help others. Her book, *The Cellars and Ceilings of Summer: An Autobiography of Trance Medium Summer Bacon*, details her miraculous journey of growing up as a mystical person and learning how to forgive and grow from all life's situations. It is one of the best personal stories I've ever read—I couldn't put the book down. In reading about her own experience, I felt closer to her. And that's what happens when we give of ourselves to others. Whether it's sharing your story in a book, sharing your time, your money, or your energy, when we give, we bridge the gap and connect with one another. When Summer shared more of herself it gave her permission to show up even more fully in the world, and in doing this, she has more friends from all over the globe, she no longer feels shy and closed off, her business has expanded, her purpose and passion are renewed, and she feels closer to her true self and to God.

When we share lessons learned from our past, we can help to uplift all those around us.

The same thing happened to me once I reached a certain level in my career. I wanted to help others by teaching what I know. Today, one of my greatest joys is my coaching and mentorship program where I work with young authors, entrepreneurs, and people ready to start their own business. After a decade of running my own business as a writer, coach, and speaker, I am able to share my knowledge, skills, talents, and what I've learned. It's fulfilling and one of the most fun parts of my business because I get to be the real me and help support others by being true to them. People want my positivity, and when I end each coaching session with a personal feel-good mantra, my clients actually want it. If I could go back to that nine-year-old who was scared to show her real self, picked on for being positive, and afraid to be seen, I'd say: "You are a gift to this world.

Be who you are, because the world needs you AS YOU ARE.

When you are true to yourself, and give yourself permission to be who you really are, your life really begins to take off."

You will arrive to a place where helping others becomes your reward. It is fulfillment in action. It doesn't always mean you need to start your own company or brand—or write your own autobiography or coach others—although if these sound joyful, then go for it. Sometimes you just want to be a stronger person for your family. It doesn't have to be some grand helping gesture. You don't have to open a wellness center to pay it forward; simply being present with your family at dinnertime, laughing, loving, and focusing on joy in the moment is grand enough. It is more about the service you offer with your intentions. This is why in all 12-step programs, the final step is to help others after you experience your own healing and growth. The final step is: *Having had a spiritual awakening as the result of these steps, we tried to carry this message to others and to practice these principles in all our affairs.* Many people become sponsors to help others along their own journey to recovery. This natural progression is demonstrated whether you are in a 12-step program or not. It is a natural urge to want to help others. Think about what you have personally gone through and how have you transformed. Where do you feel called to support others?

At this point in the journey, you may feel called to help. Anything less makes you feel you aren't expressing yourself fully. Sharing yourself can take many forms. Sometimes it's creativity and art, teaching or mentoring, volunteering, writing a book, giving of your time or money—the gift of giving.

You may even get to a place where giving is your fuel source. You will want to be of

True happiness is giving.

the highest service to others by sharing, because this is the highest form of caring. Your happiness and success will no longer be tied to what you can get, but what you can give. Life truly does become more meaningful when we follow through on our own heart's desires, be who we really are instead of who we think we need to be, and share ourselves fully with others.

Giving of your true self is not about separation or superiority, but collaboration and oneness. When you give from your heart, which is your authentic place, there is no ego or self-centeredness involved because you are giving with love.

Radical Recap

Giving is true happiness. When you heal and grow you will often get to a place where you will want to help others. This is part of personal growth and showing up more fully in your life. Your life becomes more meaningful when you share your learning with others.

AWESOME OPPORTUNITY: Participate more fully in your healing journey by sharing your true self with others.

MANTRA: "It is empowering to share more of the real me. I give to the world my true self, this is true fulfillment."

Joy Seeker Journal Time

In your workbook or joy journal, take a moment to answer these questions before progressing to the next section.

1. Where am I hiding my true self?
2. Where am I sacrificing who I really am in order to make others happy?
3. What do I love about myself?
4. Using the Real Me Pledge on the next page, make the following promise to yourself.

the Real Me Pledge

FROM HERE ON OUT...
I WILL STOP TRYING TO MAKE OTHERS HAPPY,
AT THE SACRIFICE OF MYSELF. I WILL STOP
DOWNPLAYING MY AWESOMENESS.
I KNOW I AM AMAZING AND I AM
UNAPOLOGETIC ABOUT SHINING MY LIGHT.
I WILL NO LONGER LIVE FOR OTHERS'
APPROVAL, I APPROVE OF MYSELF.
I WILL NO LONGER IDOLIZE ANYONE OR THING
NOR PUT ATTENTION ON THINGS THAT KEEP
ME FROM CONNECTING TO MY OWN DIVINE
LIGHT. I WILL BE WHO I REALLY AM,
UNAPOLOGETIC AND HAPPY. I AM PROUD OF
MYSELF AND HOW FAR I'VE COME.

I choose love and let it lead me.
I love me.

THIS IS
NOT YOUR
Practice
Life

#JoySeeker

PART 5

THE ALIGNING

How to Align with Your True Self

Your Soul Has a Statement

ALIGN WITH YOUR PURPOSE

My mission in life is not merely to survive, but to thrive.

—Maya Angelou

At this stage in our journey we've identified barriers blocking us, we've learned how to remove them, we've let go of what no longer feels good, and we are clear about what we want. We've discovered the power of self-love and expressing your true self, and we have committed to trusting ourselves and life more. And all this has led us here, to the next part of your journey, which is aligning with your true self. The stronger our relationship is with ourselves, the more confident we will be with our choices. We get confidence by being willing to do things we have never tried. This next section is about having the courage to jump forward into the unknown. We do this by trusting ourselves even more. A coaching client asked me the other day, "How certain do I need to be when making a choice, eighty percent, ninety percent, or one hundred percent?" I said, "It isn't so much about being certain, for we are never really certain because we are stepping into the unknown. But it is about knowing and trusting." You can always be certain you're making the best choice based on how you feel. Does the choice make you feel uplifted and joyful? Does it feel expansive and exciting? If we look at life like a creative adventure and see it more like a process unfolding, we can take the pressure off ourselves to make "the right" choice, and know every choice is right because we will be growing. When we make a choice, no matter what choice, we are moving ahead in life because we will be experiencing new things.

One way to feel more fulfilled in your life is to create a soul statement for yourself. Similar to a mission statement, this is a tagline for your true self expressed in the world. Creating a soul statement will help you live your values every day. A soul statement represents your desires, passion, and purpose. It is your inspiration and motivation forward. My original soul statement was: *The world is my office and I play with it daily.*

I wrote this when I first left my corporate job to follow my heart and become a writer. It represents my values because it shows that I draw inspiration from the world and I want to be location independent. I choose to play and be in wonder and never lose sight of what is most important to me: joy and connection.

Creating a soul statement helps you connect to your truest self because you have a unique point of view and set of values that are key to your own joy. And a soul statement can help you relax and enjoy your life more because it can guide you through the decision-making process; when faced with a choice, you can ask yourself which option is in line with your soul statement.

A soul statement isn't an intellectual exercise; you don't need to spend hours thinking about it and worrying if it's "right." You just need to check in with yourself and let your heart be your compass. When I first left my corporate job, I had a difficult time enjoying simple pleasures because I spent so much of my time focusing on what I was going to do next. What was my purpose? What was my passion? I spent enormous amounts of energy trying to figure out and worrying about what I was supposed to do with my life, that I was missing my actual life. After a lot of tears, trial, and error, I gracefully came to the realization that I couldn't think my way into my passion.

You can't figure out your life purpose by thinking your way into it. It can only be felt in the heart.

When we drop from our head—the frantic, "trying to figure it out," and "obsessing because we haven't yet nailed it" head—to our heart, we energetically align with our joy. We become expansive and uplift the world because we are living in our light. The feeling that something is missing is replaced with love.

The reasons soul statements work is because they connect you with your values. When you align your actions with your soul statement, everything feels easier. Get in touch with your why. Why do you want to do what you want to do? At the foundation, it should be because it brings you joy, and it makes you feel alive, excited, and connected to your best self. This is how I feel when I write. I left corporate to follow my heart, and at first I didn't know what I wanted to do, but as I put these steps into play, I started to get clear about living a beautiful life as a writer. I wrote down all the reasons I wanted to be a writer, but none of those reasons mattered as much as the one I wrote at the bottom of the page: *It makes my heart sing.* When I write I feel like my best self. When I do what I love, I feel aligned. Boom—that's all you really need. You could say all the benefits: Yes, I want to help others and be of service; I want to make a living that affords me the lifestyle I want for myself and family; I want to make more money so I can feel free. But none of that matters if you aren't having fun or connecting to your truth, which is love and joy. You don't need to put pressure on yourself about your passion and what it could or should turn into. Because doing what you love, in itself, is one of the best ways to make a difference in the world, because you are indeed putting more love into the world. We want to spend our time doing what we feel connected to because our time on earth is precious. If we don't feel joy, then what are we really doing? We certainly aren't connecting to our highest self or connecting to each other. And we aren't allowing ourselves to be who we really are. It all comes back to joy and your expression of it.

Joy Jaunt: Create a Signature Soul Statement

Creating a tagline or vision statement for yourself can be a powerful way to help you return to self when you feel out of balance.

- Identify what you value and care about.
- Use these values to create a mini tagline for yourself and your life.
- My soul statement is: _____
_____.

Radical Recap

Your purpose is to live your life with more purpose.

AWESOME OPPORTUNITY: Do what you love and what brings you joy everyday.

MANTRA: "I do what I love daily."

Drive With Your Driving Needs

ALIGN WITH YOUR VALUES

*Efforts and courage are not enough without
purpose and direction.*

—JOHN F. KENNEDY

WHEN WE DENY OURSELVES JOY and avoid acting on what makes us passion filled, we feel empty and lost inside. But you're here to experience life fully. Your life passion is part of your purpose. So many of us feel disconnected, anxious, and depressed because we are avoiding our joy. To fix this problem, we can intentionally put more joy in our life. The best method I found to do this is to start identifying your core values. What do you need in your life in order to feel like you? Think about what you value and write it down. For example, maybe you value family and spending time with loved ones. This is a good start and certainly something that brings many of us joy, but dig deeper. What is it about spending time with loved ones that you love? Maybe you love supporting others and the connection. Your value then is not necessarily just family, but connection. Another example maybe that you value nature. You feel good when you spend time outdoors, but dig a little deeper. Ask what it is about nature that you love and value. You may discover that when you are immersed in nature, you feel expressive and free. Therefore your true value is freedom. Another example: Maybe you value art or writing. You might enjoy being creative in one way or another or making things and turning your ideas into physical products. What you like is the artistic form, but your true value, once you dig a little deeper, is expressing yourself creatively. In these examples we've identified that your core values are being of service, connection, freedom, and expressing yourself creatively. These are also called your driving needs. These needs are what make you, YOU. When you align your life with them and put them at the forefront of your life, you will no longer feel depressed, anxious, or bored. Anytime you feel unbalanced or disconnected from your true self, identify how you can bring more of your driving needs into your life. These are your compass for finding and living a life full of purpose and passion.

Radical Recap

When we feel disconnected, disenchanted, depressed, anxious, or bored it is often because we are not aligned with our true self.

AWESOME OPPORTUNITY: The easiest way to stay aligned is to identify and live your values.

MANTRA: "The fastest way to fulfillment is to live my values."

Redefine Success

ALIGN WITH WHAT'S MOST IMPORTANT
TO YOU

True success is achieved by stretching oneself,
learning to feel comfortable being uncomfortable.
—Ken Poirot

I'S NICE TO HAVE GOALS based on quantifiable positive outcomes, such as a certain amount of money in the bank, an industry award or new job title, or a specific number on the scale, but these should not be what define your sense of success. A lot of people equate success with outward recognition, then define it with awards, money or fame, social media numbers, sales goals, and so forth, when this doesn't really have much to do with real success in life. First of all, sometimes numbers are really meaningless. I know of some widely successful coaches and authors who choose to go off social media and their business is thriving, and I know other coaches and authors who have hundreds of thousands of followers on social media but can barely pay their bills. I know people whose net worth is off the charts and are still living a life from a place of scarcity, while others may have a more modest income and live a truly prosperous, fulfilling, and abundant life. It isn't the quantity that is important, it is the quality. When your life is aligned with your core values, that is true success.

The first few years of my business I was really consumed with numbers. I was so focused on my social media numbers, thinking that meant success. A good day was defined by how many likes I got, and I was thrown into fits of worry and self-doubt when the numbers didn't come in. I watched my book rankings at online retailers obsessively, and considered anything less than a five-star review a dismal failure. I set financial goals based on what I imagined other coaches and authors were earning, and felt pressured to constantly be making more. As you can imagine, this thinking didn't work so well. I was stressed and exhausted all the time, working feverishly trying to do more, but not really getting anywhere and never feeling like I was enough. I was very much in my head and driven by fear. This was before I understood my worth and thought my value came from what I do. It was my fear-based mind that was attached to the numbers. I'd think, *I've been doing my business for two to three years. I should have more people attend my workshops. What am I doing wrong?*

We know that everything is energy, even our thoughts. Well this energy kept clients and potential book buyers away. But change happened when I realigned with my soul statement, redefined success, and visualized my ideal outcome. I let go of my attachment to what I thought success was and instead turned my focus to gratitude and service. I started to say to the Universe, my higher power, "Thank you for this beautiful life. I get to express myself and do what I love daily. I am so grateful for all that is well in my life. And the people who are part of my community." This became my mantra, and nothing shy of miracles started to happen. I landed a book deal for my first traditionally published book, *mindbodygreen*, reached out to be a course leader, and my social media presence grew naturally and quite fast. How did this all happen? Because I shifted my focus to joy and gratitude instead of lack and frustration. I aligned with what brought me joy—the joy of writing, the joy of living, the joy of being happy, the joy of helping others—instead of focusing on numbers or recognition. I reframed how I defined success and I became abundant, confident, and secure. By turning to joy, my business grew without pressure or effort. Let go of how it's supposed to look and let the joy lead you forward.

Joy is the best barometer for success.

When we can shift our perception out of lack and fear into joy and love, that is when we will experience true miracles for our life. Choose love as the highest form of success. Instead of asking for more followers, more likes, more clients, more money, ask for more trust and faith in your journey. Ask to trust that you are right where you are supposed to be, and you will be given the right guidance and insight to move forward in a path that is for your highest good. The only thing for you to do is celebrate where you are right now and release the focus on needing more. That is the truest form of success.

Radical Recap

Success is not about a job title, more money, or more social media followers. All of that is fleeting.

Real success is about how you feel and being true to yourself by honoring joy. Lasting success is the inner peace within.

AWESOME OPPORTUNITY: Take time to redefine success and what you value and care about in life.

MANTRA: "I am a success because I am full of joy."

Joy Seeker Journal Time

In your joy journal, take a moment to answer these questions before progressing to the next section.

1. Where have I been trying to control the outcome?
2. What are my core values and driving needs?
3. What does success mean to me?

YOUR
Dreams
ARE THE
SIGNATURE
TO YOUR
Potential

#JoySeeker

PART 6

THE ACTUALIZING

How to Create and Step into Your Ideal Life

Your Dream Is
Your Destiny

——

STEP INTO YOUR CURIOSITY

*Desire is a teacher: When we immerse ourselves
in it without guilt, shame, or clinging, it can
show us something special about our own minds
that allows us to embrace life fully.*

—MARK EPSTEIN

ONE OF MY FAVORITE QUESTIONS to ask people is: What is your biggest dream? What do you really want to do? In this next section, your dreams pave the way forward. When we give ourselves permission to dream, we feel more connected to our authentic self.

This part of our journey can be liberating, intoxicating, and one of the most intense and exciting times of all. You may soon discover a power within you that gives your life new energy and focus, and you feel a deeper connection to yourself and your divine purpose. The work you've done up until this point really begins to pay off. As you see the results manifest, you will become even more motivated to keep going and moving forward. The reason this phase feels so good is because we are finally trusting ourselves and leading more with faith. We begin to let go of the outcome and surrender to the process. In this section you will learn how to break away from what you think you need to do, to step into all you are truly *meant* to do.

Soon everything else revolves around your joy because your true self discovers happiness is in pursuit of what makes you happiest.

By now, you likely recognize where you've been giving away your power. You may be excited to take a gigantic leap. The dreams that you've held in your heart for months, years, decades are in full throttle. It's starting to feel impossible to play small in your life. You no longer are content to settle. Once you get crystal clear on what you want, making it happen becomes so much easier. When you are aligned with who you truly are, and you make a choice, the Universe swoops in to support you. But first we have to believe in the power of our choices, and we must recognize that everything we want is possible. It is a beautiful life when you dedicate yourself to being true to yourself in pursuit of your dreams.

Get very clear within yourself: What do you desire? Now is the time to see this gorgeous dream through.

The amazing thing about this exciting time in your life is now more than ever you see how important your dreams are and you know they matter. My lifelong dream to travel the world was birthing all kinds of new clarity. Remember everything has a vibration, including our dreams and even places. As I was traveling the world, I kept meeting people who would ask me, *What's next?* What are you going to do when your year of travel and being on the move is over? Whenever they asked, I felt a tinge of excitement because I didn't know, which meant my future was full of possibilities. The unknown no longer scared me as I saw it as part of embracing a fulfilled life. This showed growth, because I used to obsess about the future and thought I needed everything planned out. There was a time in my life when I needed to know the outcome. I had a five-, ten- and twenty-year plan. But when milestones passed and my plans didn't pan out, I felt like a failure, and a loser, which made me reconsider everything I thought I wanted. Clearly, this wasn't working, so my new approach to life is, "Wait and see." When people ask what's next, I simply smile and say, "I guess we have to wait and see." This response usually freaks some people out. That's the thing with society: There is an incredible amount of pressure we put on ourselves and each other. When we go into college, people want to know what our major is. When we graduate, people need to know what we are going to do. When we start dating, people ask when we are getting married. And when we get married soon people ask when the kiddos are coming. It never really ends. The pressure and expectations pushed on us are overwhelming. And this idea, that life is set for us and we are on a specific plan, can be frustrating—especially when our life doesn't fall into place, making us feel like we are off track.

The reality is there is no one master plan, and happiness isn't about conforming to someone else's expectations. Once again, the key is in connecting to your true self. When you follow through on the inspiration that comes to you, the right plan for you will reveal itself. You see, each dream we pursue will give us more clarity into the next phase of our life, but we must step forward into our dreams and go forth into the unknown in order to get this clarity. And the unknown is where the true magic can happen.

In diving fully into my own Joy Seeker Journey, I was searching for my next dream. I didn't tell anyone at the time, but part of me traveling the world for an entire year was to hopefully find a place I could call home. I always saw myself splitting my time between countries, but had yet to find a place I loved enough to actually live in. But all of that changed when I arrived in Barcelona. I had found a place I truly loved. It felt like time stopped and happiness flooded through my entire being. I knew within the first hour of arriving that this was my new favorite place on earth. I said out loud to myself in the back of the taxi, "I am going to come back to Barcelona and stay longer." It was my dream date with my destiny. I had a glimpse into my new dream. That's the thing about dreams: Once we start living them, they carve a path for new ones to be realized. These are your secret admirers, a future destination, a dream yet to be lived, that is designed specifically for you. Dreams have their own energy. And you have dreams waiting for you, but we can't meet up with them until we see the current dream through to its completion. We need to take action on the ones in our heart now in order to meet up with our fullest expression of happiness, which lies in the unmet dreams waiting for us.

Follow through on the inspiration in your heart. That is the only way to meet the fullest, most authentic version of your true self.

My trip around the world led to me wanting even more of Barcelona. Whether I go back to visit or live there for three months or a year, it doesn't matter. I just know I will go back. Having things to look forward to, combined with the "Wait and See" mentality, will grace your life with peace, wonder, and awe. However, you need to let your dreams unfold. Once I arrived in Barcelona, I felt like I had met my soul mate place. And when you meet the love of your life, you want the rest of your life to start right now. I was only four months into my Joy Seeker Journey, but I thought about abandoning it all to trade in my old dream for this new fresh shiny one. Maybe you can relate, most of us do this. We take action on our dreams, and as we step forth on the path, we soon see other things that grab our attention. We sometimes doubt ourselves and wonder if we can really pull it off. Maybe the current dream is harder than we thought, or maybe we just lose momentum. Sometimes it's not at all what we expected.

When new ideas and goals pop up, this is the Universe's way of guiding us. It's not always meant for us to jump ship and abandon the current path right away. Look at your inspirations like secret admirers. They are future dreams showing you what's possible. They plant seeds and guide you to fulfillment.

I saw so clearly my life in Barcelona, my own apartment, my routine, a dog, the city, and I deeply engaged in a passionate love affair. I knew this was my *dream destiny*, my dream yet to be actualized. But if I left one dream prematurely before it was fully mature and actualized, I would always have that gnawing nudge, that "what if" feeling, and the "what might have been" sensation would definitely haunt me forever. If I ended my trip around the world after four months to settle in Barcelona prematurely, I would be abandoning a piece of me that needed to see the dream I was living through as far as I could. To be honest, my current dream was pretty sweet. I was traveling the world full-time. Why would I want to change directions? But this is the dreamer process. We step into a dream, no matter how big or small it is, and new opportunities show up. And many of us think about changing course. Maybe things don't look the way we thought they would, or we just see something else we want. But leaving our dream prematurely can leave a part of us hanging, always wondering what could have been.

So, how do we know if the new dream is our heart guiding us, or if we're jumping ship too soon? The idea is to live a regret-free life, which means you make choices from a place of love and joy versus lack and worry. When you make choices that you know are aligned with who you truly are, you will always know which direction to go. Sure, moving to Barcelona would be exciting, but that excitement from new dreams always fades. Then we wonder about the piece of us in our past that never saw the thing we wanted most all the way through. "Don't live with regrets. Keep going"—that's what I told myself. When we trade dreams before we see them through, we end up losing faith in ourselves and don't learn to not trust our own judgments.

Part of building your life on a solid foundation is to keep your promises to yourself. The result of abandoning your dreams prematurely means you abandon a piece of yourself.

When you have a dream and go for it, you are keeping your word to yourself. It isn't so much about how it turns out, but the process of living that dream that is the most important thing. When we abandon our dreams mid-path, for whatever reason—fear of failure, not enough support, a new dream seems more exciting—we are abandoning a part of our true self. I think one of the tricks to staying on course with our dreams is to let go of how we think it should look and just trust the process and unfolding. There is a period of our manifestation process when we are living our dreams and we become a more complete version of ourselves. If this hasn't happened yet, you will sell yourself short. In this space of self-actualization, we learn more about what we truly need and want. When this happens we may get to a point where the current dream can no longer serve us, and it will be time to reevaluate. But before that point, it is important to see the dream through as far as you can. As long as it feels good keep going.

Think about a dream of yours that you ended early. Do you still wonder what would have been? What new life can you give to old projects or dreams? If it is still on your mind it could be worth pursuing again.

Even after falling in love with Barcelona, I knew with every fiber of my body that the Joy Seeker Journey must continue. I needed to keep traveling. The dream had to unfold one day at a time. Dreams that are meant to be followed will stay close in your heart until it is their time to be lived. My Barcelona dream is still there in my future, waiting for the right time for me to pursue it.

Imagine that our dreams are like us. They are living, breathing things that want love and attention. They need us to live through them as we grow. As you grow, your dreams do, too. The key thing about our dreams is not the destination but who we become in the process. Dreams are meant to be lived fully, in the moment, and when we do so, we become more of who we are meant to be, we become more of our truest self.

When we change and grow, so do our dreams.

When we grow into the next level of ourselves, we may outgrow our dreams. So how do we know if a dream is worth following through on or if it is time to readjust? In my life coaching practice, I've identified three different types of dreamers.

1. The No Goers: Don't know their dreams
2. The Comfort Goers: Know their dreams but don't want to realize them
3. The Actualizers: Know their dreams and are actively pursuing them

Let's dive into each.

THE NO GOERS. These are people who don't know what their dreams are. At least this is how it seems. They are afraid to know their dreams because that truth changes everything. They may be in a situation that is comfortable. It pays the bills, keeps them safe, they are able to get by. If they went inward to seek their own truth, that could mean massive change. Change is not something easily managed, so they opt for ignoring their inner calling and choose to not follow their destiny. It is too risky, too unpredictable, too scary to think about, so they don't think about it. They know something is missing in their life, but they are perfectly okay with just going through the motions because it gives them security.

This scenario can play out in all areas of our life. I had a life coaching client who was a no goer for decades. She was in an unhappy, emotionally abusive relationship and felt stuck in every area of her life. She was terrified of dreaming because that would mean rocking the boat of her expected existence. When I asked her what she wanted, for months she said she didn't know. This is the way of the no goers. They do have dreams, for we all do, but they won't be able to tell you what they are because they don't consciously allow themselves to know. Because realizing the idea of the dream would require change, and changing means growing and going into the unknown, which is not something they are prepared to face. But we all get to a point like my coaching client, where our unhappiness is no longer an option. We choose joy, and the pursuit of our goal is of the upmost importance for our own sanity.

THE COMFORT GOERS. These are people who often have emerged from the no goers category and realize that maybe they can be happier and it starts with getting clear about what they want. The people who are in this category are often aware of their dreams. They sometimes daydream about a better way of being—maybe changing jobs, relationships, locations, or using their money to invest in a new venture—but they don't really see themselves taking action on the dream. They are used to just going through the motions. They have worked hard to create a level of success, structure, and security and don't want to rock the boat. Going for that dream that they think about all the time means change, and they are so comfortable with where they are that they tell themselves it's okay.

When my coaching client arrived at this phase, she couldn't hold back anymore. She excitedly told me she's always wanted to have a cottage by the sea. Her lack of clarity and being afraid to admit what she wanted was suddenly replaced with an exciting energy that fueled her forward. I asked her what steps she needs to take to get there, and she was unable to think about action steps for it seemed too treacherous.

The comfort goers may know what they want but they aren't motivated to act on their dreams. They are more attached to comfort and want to avoid risk. They enjoy thinking about what might be. Going for what they want requires a dedication to the unknown. They say things like, "I will do that dream in the next chapter of my life, when I retire/graduate/have more money/when the kids are out of school/in my next life." The dream is put on hold because today is comfortable and safe. Today is manageable; it is predictable. They can deal with the current situation, even if it makes them unhappy, because it is safe. It isn't that the dream scares them as it did for the no goers. It is that the life they are living is so comfortable that they don't see a reason to change. The difference is they have moved from fear to complacency.

THE ACTUALIZERS. Eventually we get to a place where we can no longer hide our true selves, we burst into actualizing our dreams, and soon enough everything feels better. Welcome to the club. This is the group who are very aware of their dreams and they are actively pursuing them. There is a point where we want more for ourselves and loved ones. We realize that life is meant to be lived and lived more deeply, so we trade in our limiting belief that security and comfort provide happiness and instead opt for courage and risk, because that is where growth happens.

About a year after working with my coaching client, we stopped our sessions together. She went from being a no goer to a comfort goer and that was that, until she came to one of my retreats. I'll never forget the day she pulled me aside and said, "I did it. I left my husband and am living in a cottage by the sea. I am happier than I've ever been." We hugged and celebrated her true self. She was now living her dream life and connected to her authentic joy.

My client was able to recognize her dream because she discovered how important it is to put herself first. The actualizers live deeply, feel fully, and open their hearts immensely wide to possibilities. They are taking steps daily to make their dreams come true

We know what will make us happy. It's walking away from all the things that don't make us happy that is the initial challenge.

and they love living with joy. They enjoy dreaming and seeing their goals manifest into reality.

In pursuing your dreams, you live out your highest potential. Think about your deepest desire and identify where you are on the dreamer spectrum. The goal is to live your life as an actualizer, because that's where joy, possibilities, and wonder live.

Radical Recap

Your dreams are part of your happiness and potential. The things that you think about are part of your destiny.

AWESOME OPPORTUNITY: Follow through on your dreams and happiness will be yours.

MANTRA: "My dreams are the signature to my potential. I trust them and follow through."

Everyone Has
a Barcelona

———

STEP INTO YOUR DEEPEST DESIRES

I look at the human life like an experiment.
Every new moment, every new experience, tragic
or otherwise, is an opportunity to gain a more
accurate perspective and helps lead me to clarity.
—STEVE GLEASON

As I've illustrated, dreams are born within each other. Once you live out a dream, it makes way for the next. Just like me living my Joy Seeker Journey, traveling full-time, led me to realize I want to be in Barcelona for an extended period of time. We must pursue each dream, as they are the catalyst for growth and new awareness.

Consider your dreams stepping-stones to your highest potential. As long as we live a life dedicated to them, we are living our potential. A life lived in pursuit of your dreams is rewarding, deep, and meaningful. Why? Because you feel more connected to yourself and others. But don't forget that your dreams are for you. You don't need others to approve of them for you to go after them. But for many of us, when there is a lack of support, we start to second-guess our dreams.

The third day I was in Barcelona, completely soaked up in a love affair with the city, I met an American couple at a restaurant. They were sitting at the table next to me, and hearing the familiar American accents, I initiated a conversation with them. I asked how they were enjoying Barcelona. They looked at each other with sheer frustration and disgust and told me they hated it. Of all the places they traveled to in Spain, they thought Barcelona was underwhelming, and they couldn't wait to leave. I thought to myself, *How can anyone hate the most amazing city on the planet? I love this place.* There I was trying to figure out how to continue the bliss of Barcelona, and these folks were desperate to escape. Then something happened that was very surprising to me. As we sipped sangria, I started to second-guess my own dream. I wondered if they were right. Did they see something I didn't see? Was I just in the honeymoon phase, seeing everything with rose-colored glasses?

When we believe others' point of view about our dreams, we will second-guess ourselves and lose faith in our desires. I tried to look at the same city I loved so much through a tinted lens of disapproval. I thought, *What do they know that I don't?* Interestingly enough, I questioned my own beliefs but not theirs. And most of us do this. We get excited about a new idea, we share it with people, and our enthusiasm is hardly ever met with the same excitement. Then we don't feel supported, so we start to second-guess ourselves and our dreams. But when we realize our dreams are for us and no one else, then we will bring our power back. It wasn't until I remembered that not everyone is supposed to have the same dream and I stopped second-guessing myself.

Your dreams are for you. It is your own soul language. It's perfectly okay that two strangers from America don't have the same dream as I do, my second-guessing was an ego trick. That's what our fear does. It tries to latch on to others' opinions to make us feel as if our opinions are not good enough. It will do everything it can to convince us that we shouldn't continue on our path. It will say, "Trade in your dream, it's no good." Don't buy in to the fear. When I was able to recognize that my second-guessing was fear based, I was able to feel once again the grand love I had for Barcelona. In that moment I brought my power back and vowed to myself to never let someone else's opinion stir me away from my own truth.

When we are living our truth and actively pursuing our desires, others will not always agree or understand. But remember, this is your own truth—no one else's. Your dreams are for you. And here is what you really need to know: You can choose to love and honor your own light and joy, or you can choose fear. You can walk in light or dark. You get to choose.

Having goals and living out your dreams is the most beautiful gift you can give yourself, but the magic, the true joy and the fulfilling aspect of it comes when you can share it with others.

Having a supportive partner or family members who can live your dreams with you is wonderful, but sometimes we don't have people in our lives who want the same things we do. I knew my dream was to travel the world, but before I left, I didn't know anyone else who was in a position to do that, too. I invited my family, my best friends, even people I recently met, because I wanted to share my joy and the experience with others. But no one else in my life was able to join. But the urge to share was insatiable because the dream to travel wasn't just for me. I wanted to share it with others. I needed a connection. We may think living for ourselves or going after what we want is selfish, but usually those who don't go after what they want feel this way. For those who live from their heart know that going after what you want is not just about you and your own happiness but uplifting the entire world. Because when you help yourself, you help inspire others. Truthfully you see that life is so much better together. The connection is a foundational part of living a fulfilled life, and we get this need met by reaching out to others and by sharing more of who we truly are. I realized this when my mom flew out to visit me in Prague. For almost five months I had been traveling solo, and her company was refreshing. It reminded me how important family is and how special it is to share your dreams with others. It was so much more rewarding to see the city and explore with her.

I learned the value of real connection and had a deep desire to share my experiences, so I took my dream online and shared my journey openly on social media. I was able to connect with people all around the world—in real life while traveling, but also online by sharing my journey with them. This helped me build up a solid community and feel more fulfilled because the dream wasn't just for me. It became a movement, a message much bigger than me. That is where the real fulfillment comes in: when we share our dreams openly and honestly with others. Whether you share your dreams with close loved ones or publicly online, sharing is caring and it is an essential part of living a fulfilled life. The bottom line is everyone has their own "Barcelona," the dream in our heart that inspires us and brings immense joy. Be true to yourself and honor your unique form of happiness and you will be able to connect with like-minded people.

Joy Jaunt: Connect with Others

Connection is at the core of our happiness. When we connect to others, we feel more purposeful, so this week take some time to connect with others about your dreams and goals. Do you have a soul sister or mister who can help support your vision? Do you have an idea, a project, or personal belief you'd like to share with others? Maybe call up a friend and meet them for coffee, spend time sharing your true self and connecting with loved ones. Challenge yourself to share more of who you really are. Share your dreams openly and ask how you can support one another.

Radical Recap

Not everyone will understand your dreams, and that is okay. Your dreams are for you. When you pursue them, you show up for yourself and this brings more light into the world.

AWESOME OPPORTUNITY: Focus on what inspires you and your joy. Your happiness will inspire others and help to uplift them as well.

MANTRA: "My dreams are for me and honoring them is joy."

Joy Seeker Journal Time

In your joy journal, take a moment to answer these questions before progressing to the next section.

1. Where have I been doubting myself or listening to the opinions of others?
2. What does my ideal life feel like?
3. What dream is in my heart of hearts?
4. What guided action will I take today to follow through on this desire?

WE LeaRN THE WAY ON THE Way

#JoySeeker

PART 7

THE ALLOWING

How to Trust Yourself and Life

Limited Limitations

——

TRUST YOUR INSTINCTS

When I let go of what I am, I become what I might be.

—Lao Tzu

A T THIS POINT IN YOUR JOURNEY, you've been doing the work. You've been showing up for yourself and following through on your dreams. You've been listening to the guidance and applying the tools and seeing great results. You feel happier, healthier, and more connected. But it always seems to happen: You're feeling good and, seemingly out of nowhere, the rug is pulled out from under you. It feels like things are breaking up, breaking down, and falling apart. When this happens many of us question the world. We regret and resent things we once enjoyed and start to think it was all for nothing. Most often, this happens when we focus on how we think it's supposed to look. But what's really happening is our insecurities, old beliefs, patterns, and habits that have not been completely healed are coming to the surface. We've grown and vibrated higher, so anything not addressed within us that is still holding us back will reveal itself. It is normal in this part of our journey to feel confused that you aren't further along. You may even become irritated, impatient, and angry. Know that this is all part of the growth cycle. This phase cannot be skipped over or rushed. Focus forward with grace and ease as you allow the awareness needed to heal yourself for good to move you forward.

When things seem to be falling apart, they are actually falling into place. Trust the process.

When I was in Vilnius, Lithuania, I spent an entire day dedicated to looking for the best view of the city. According to my map, there were a couple different locations for great views. But as I approached each one, I was severely let down. One was closed for construction, and the other wasn't accessible at all. After hours of wandering aimlessly around the city, I felt like throwing in the towel. But I decided to push a little bit further and chose to give it one more shot. By the time I actually arrived to the third viewpoint, I was exhausted. My legs felt like rubber and my body just wanted to return to bed. I looked up the staircase in front of me and saw another fenced off area. My mind raced to all the reasons it was a bad idea to continue forward:

- It didn't work in the past.
- It won't be worth it.
- You can use your time more wisely in another way.

- Your life really won't be any different if you do go for it.
- This is just another path that won't lead to anything.

I was ready to give up and call it a day. But, although I didn't know it at the time, this was a true teaching moment for me.

If we are open in our journey, we learn the deeper life lessons that our soul needs for its full actualization and expression. When you dive into a life dedicated to being true to yourself, you will come face-to-face with areas of yourself that have yet to be healed. There will be moments that trigger us and make us second-guess everything. All of our doubts and self-imposed limitations that we have yet to look at will start to surface, but this is so we can look at them and heal them once and for all. If you are happy and living a life dedicated to your dreams but you have yet to address your deepest insecurities, then you can't be fully fulfilled. Something will always feel a little off. We need to heal any wounds that have been blocking us from feeling contentment and inner peace. Now we have the opportunity to visit the parts of ourselves that need the most love and attention.

The doubt that creeps in during this phase is different from the doubt we felt before. Early in our Joy Seeker Journey, we doubted our ability. We weren't quite sure if we could pull it off. But here we are now, pulling it off, we are living our dreams, but it feels different from what we thought. So the doubt is pushed onto our dreams. *Is this all there is? Did I waste my time and energy to get here?* And this new self-doubt makes us question everything in our life. This is an excavation; deep issues will pop up, so they can be healed for good. Old relationship wounds, grief from the past, and unhealed insecurities are now at the forefront of your life. They are in your face because they can no longer be ignored. In order to get to the next phase of your life, these limitations must be understood so they can be removed, for they are the final things holding you back. Pema Chordron said, "Nothing ever goes away until it has taught us what we need to know." This unsettled time is you healing and learning and recognizing things you didn't even know were holding you back.

This can be a painful time in our life, but only when we resist. It's difficult only when we think our life is supposed to look a different way. When we can surrender fully to the experience, we can invite grace in to help heal the situation. Things feel frustrating and awkward because you are emerging into a newer version of yourself. You are living at a new level. You are doing things you've never done before, so it can be uncomfortable because it's new. This newness presents new thoughts, ideas, and situations. You are asked to go deeper into who you really are and what you really want.

As I looked up that hill in Lithuania, I thought about turning back and abandoning my goal to find the best view of the city. The hill in front of me looked so large and it would have been easier to abort the mission. But as my mind was scheming ways to turn back, my feet were stepping forward. One step at a time, I was moving toward my goal. As I climbed the hill, I said to myself, "You're committed to this. You are going to see this through." As I was climbing, I realized it wasn't even about the view. Sure, that's what I thought I wanted, or so said the stubborn part of me that was on a mission to find a perfect photo spot. But as I thought more about this venture, it became a metaphor for my entire trip. It was each step I took along the way that was the most important. It was about being present with the feelings that were emerging in the journey. With each step, it was pushing me further along in my life. Actually, this entire day was a huge metaphor for all of life. We get to power through or surrender to what is. We can look at our situations as a huge waste and when things don't turn out as planned, we can think we are off track. Or we can see everything as a joyous experiment and see the power of being fully in the journey is the truest sense of happiness and peace.

At any point on our Joy Seeker Journey we can turn back, change course, or keep going. And there is no wrong choice. All of it is just life and how we want to live. Living a life committed to joy is not an easy one. It requires courage and honesty. It will push you against your edge, all in an attempt to reveal your truest, healthiest, happiest self. That is the real mission we are on. To be fulfilled, connected, and aligned. And any brave journey will ask us to dig deep and access parts of us we didn't know existed. This is the way of the Joy Seeker. It requires courage but it is the most authentic way to live.

With each step I took up that massive hill, I was closer to a new reality. I was growing, and I was expanding myself and my point of view. As I climbed, I decided not to look back. I didn't want to get distracted or worse, lose motivation, so I kept my head down and put one foot in front of the other. One step at a time, one moment at a time, I climbed. And when I got to the top of the hill, it suddenly all made sense. There I was, my legs even more tired, my body sweaty, and my brain racing with thoughts. But in that moment of looking out over the gorgeous city, I felt it: I felt the peace that comes with following through. There I was gazing out. It was the most beautiful view of the city. But it isn't what I saw that made this moment so spectacular. It was how I felt. I was accomplished. I kept a promise to myself and I saw this vision through, and that is what made this outcome so rewarding. My previous attempts at finding the perfect view were not successful. But I kept going despite the obstacles.

We all have outcomes that we want, but the most important things are that we keep the promises to ourselves and honor our true self along the way. The promise to ourselves is a commitment to joy. You will get to a place in your life where the promise to yourself will outweigh the outcome or the goal you thought you wanted. And as I sat there on top of the hill taking in my entire journey, I had the clarity to revise my master plan.

Radical Recap

Your dreams are important and worth seeing through.

AWESOME OPPORTUNITY: Commit to joy and let the joy guide you.

MANTRA: "I trust myself and follow through on the inspiration from my heart."

Radical Trust

TRUST THE FUTURE

Dear past, thanks for all the lessons. Dear future,
I'm ready...

—Unknown

HALFWAY THROUGH LIVING MY DREAM—spending 365 days traveling the world—I had an epiphany. I recognized that I was putting a lot of pressure on my experience. I wanted and expected that my experience would bring me unlimited bliss. I thought traveling would be my golden ticket to happiness, you know like finding the pot of gold at the end of the rainbow. But as I dived in fully, I soon learned it was just travel. It's not humanity, connection, true joy, or fulfillment. The real magic is what happens on the inside of you when you follow through on your own true desires. Once I realized this, I was able to tap into more joy by seeing that what I really craved was not from the experiences but what I brought to the experiences.

So I made a bold decision. I changed directions and decided to end my trip early. The reason the choice to end my trip felt so good is because I knew I was being true to myself. I was continuing to follow my heart and trust the unfolding of life. As I let go of expectations, this allowed me to grow gracefully and transition into the next chapter of my life with confidence, ease, and joy.

It may sound like I'm contradicting myself because a few pages ago I said it's important to follow through on your dream. But let me be clear: We should always follow through on the dream in our heart, but it is vitally important to recognize if our dream continues to be heart based.

Just like a child growing up, when we grow emotionally and spiritually, there will be growing pains. What's really happening is the cleansing and release of a false self. It is a letting go of the parts of us that are no longer needed. We are being groomed to be fully realized. Our fullest expression, the happiest, healthiest, most authentic version of ourselves, is trying to emerge. Think of the fall time when trees let go of leaves, they are releasing parts of themselves so they can grow and change with the season.

What also happens is that we transform. Like the caterpillar turning into a butterfly, we are evolving and growing into the next phase of our journey, getting ever closer to who we are at our core. And this requires an inner strength that I call radical trust. Trust in yourself, the future, and the Universe. One way to do this is to celebrate how far you've come. Think about how far you have come on this journey. You know you are farther along because:

- You recognized and identified your dreams.
- You are actively manifesting your deepest desires.

- You've dived headfirst into and experienced it for all it has to offer.
- You now know what you truly need.
- You have a deeper connection to yourself and others.
- You trust yourself more.

In this phase, not only do we have more clarity and confidence, but we understand ourselves more. And we've made promises to ourselves based on past lessons we've learned. So the dreams that once brought you joy may no longer give you the same fulfillment. Like my dream to travel that faded. Now it was time to trust the unfolding and next phase of life. And guess what, my dear? That is perfectly okay. It's actually part of your journey. This is what living a fulfilled life actually looks like. Changing your mind and going with the flow of your own life based on the inspiration you feel within.

The goal is to align with your true self. It comes back to trusting yourself. This is the path of the brave, wild Joy Seeker—to commit to a life that honors who you are at a soul level, in each and every moment of your life. Don't be afraid to change directions; your true self is asking you to grow.

A change of heart is nothing more than allowing yourself to be who you really are. It's about growing into the next level you.

When I finally was able to see what my journey was all about, I reached that conclusion that my dream to travel full-time had an expiration date sooner than I had anticipated. I had originally committed to traveling for a full year, but when it wasn't feeling right, I needed to adjust and re-center. I would be lying if I said I didn't worry about changing course at first. I worried I was giving up, falling short. I had invested so much in this dream and now, was I just going to walk away? Plus, I was documenting my journey on social media; what would everyone think? But then I remembered that it doesn't matter what anyone thinks, and the real point of the journey was coming back to myself.

The Universe was giving me the opportunity to own my worth and get clear about what is truly most important to me. Do I stay in a situation that no longer feels in alignment, expansive or joyful because I already invested time and money? Do I worry about being judged or ridiculed? Or do I follow my joy route and choose self-love and fulfillment? Remembering the promise I made to myself, I continued to follow my heart and let joy lead.

The most important thing is how you feel, and you want to choose experiences that make you feel good. If you are in a situation that is suffocating your soul or you feel unsafe, uninspired, and unmotivated, it is an opportunity to take stock and see what new direction will be more fulfilling.

When we seek to reach new goals, it's because we want to feel good. But when we get into a situation in our life that no longer feels good, we have to give ourselves permission to reexamine, revaluate, and, if we feel guided to, change directions.

For me, feeling good meant going home. Choosing joy meant realigning to be close to loved ones, the place I belonged. In giving myself what I needed the most, without fear of failure, without overanalyzing my choice, without worrying about other opinions, I was honoring my true self. This is the ultimate way of the Joy Seeker, to be true to yourself no matter what. Everything becomes more peaceful and awe inspired when you dedicate yourself to this new way of life.

We set out on this entire experience to become who we are meant to be, to connect to our true self, to live our highest potential. This means trusting yourself fully

True joy is trusting ourselves and the process of life.

and aligning with what feels right in each and every moment. Joy Seeking is about living in complete accordance with who you are at a soul level.

Joy isn't something you chase. It is something within you already. It is you—your essence and core is joy. Once I discovered the joy was me, I wanted to take my joy to the people I loved most, my family and close friends. Home was calling me because I had found my home in my heart. True belonging is a connection within yourself with your heart.

What's really happening at this phase in our life is we have emerged into a truer version of ourselves as we trust ourselves more than ever. In this new awareness, we are more connected to our heart, which connects us closer to the Universe. The joy that was within us all along can finally show up more fully. And when we

When you are true to yourself, you are joy in the highest expression.

make choices from this aligned place, everything flows much easier. Your life becomes a gorgeous masterpiece.

We can start to see that our illusions, the ones that used to try to take control, have no power over us anymore. The worries like, *What will people think? Am I off track? Did I make a mistake?* don't even resonate anymore. What we once believed to be true falls away as our old limitations have been replaced with love and awareness. We feel more courageous and powerful as we make our choices from a place of power and confidence versus weakness and doubt. This is such a beautiful time because hope, courage, and confidence lead the way. We've been hopeful before, but this feeling, at this point in the journey, is much different. This time it is from a deeper part of our being, where we get even more honest and real about who we are and what we want for ourselves and loved ones. We now know what we need for our own well-being and we will not sacrifice any part of us or settle. The reason this phase feels so magical is because we step back a bit to see that everything truly is in divine order. It's all part of your own creation, your master plan, your beautiful novel or masterpiece.

How do we get to a place where we feel so empowered? We lean into radical trust by letting faith lead us. We dive so fully into our life and let go of all expectations, all compromises, all judgments, for we know at the core of our being we are the master of our life when we align with our higher self and source energy. We get to create whatever we want, and that brings a newfound freedom that is unshakable. The entire Joy Seeker Journey is about you becoming who you really are. It is part something you reveal, and part something you create.

We are the creators of our own life experience.

You will arrive to a place in your journey where you see the best thing to do is to give yourself what you need at a soul level. And sometimes that is completely opposite of what you anticipated at the beginning. When you make all your choices from a heart-centered place, your ego cannot manipulate you. The judgment and shame you once felt has been replaced with contentment, inner peace, and clarity.

Welcome to the true you. This is one of the most light-filled, happy, healthy, and joyous times of your life. You don't second-guess yourself, and you are unapologetic about who you are. This is when you get to spread your wings and soar above the past pains, above the drama, and into highest form of happiness. You are now living a life with massive meaning. Every choice you make from here on out is aligned with who you are at the core of your being, so each step of your journey is more graceful and purposeful.

Radical Recap

The real magic is what happens on the inside of you when you follow through on your own true desires. When you change your mind and go with the flow of your own life based on the inspiration you feel everything becomes more joyful. True joy is trusting ourselves and the process of life.

AWESOME OPPORTUNITY: When you know yourself you trust and believe in yourself. Focus on personal growth, self-awareness and self-love.

MANTRA: "I am the joy I seek"

Radical Reset

——

TRUST THE JOURNEY

Some people believe holding on and hanging in there are signs of great strength. However, there are times when it takes much more strength to know when to let go and then do it.

—ANN LANDERS

I SHARED THE POWER OF following through and seeing our ideas and dreams to completion, but completion isn't always the finish line. When we are honest with ourselves, listening to our heart, and trusting the process, we may be surprised by the outcome. For sometimes, the dreams we dive into will show us more of who we truly are and give us what we need faster than we anticipated. When this happens the ending will almost always look different than we expect.

By now, you are beginning to understand what joy means to you. You thought it would be in achieving your goal or living out your dream, but perhaps you are doing that and fulfillment still eludes you. This is because you are stuck in between the place you thought you wanted to be and the place you no longer feel good in. The key is to take a look around and take stock. To question who you really are and what that really means.

I was confronted by this need to recalibrate while I was traveling around the world. I thought traveling was my number one passion and it would make me happy. But for the majority of my trip, I wasn't actually happy. In fact, I was frustrated, stressed, and challenged—emotionally, physically, and spiritually. There were many days I questioned what I was doing, and there were many tears along with the questions. Upon reflection, I realized I also experienced moments of pure wonder, beauty, grace, gratitude, love, and awe on my trip. And I finally came to the conclusion that what I was searching for and found was much deeper than just being happy. I wanted to live and feel my life fully. I discovered a sense of purpose, connection, how to live a life with more meaning. I learned that what matters most to me is connecting with loved ones, family, friends, having a sense of community, being part of something bigger than yourself... belonging. For me, this is fulfillment, this is inner peace.

It really shocked me to realize that travel couldn't make me happy. However, I discovered that if we do it right, it will show us what will. Experiencing new cultures is exciting, challenging, and keeps us locked into consistent aha moments, but I've learned that "traveling" isn't just moving from one place to another. It is the movement that happens in your heart. Genuine travel is what really happens on the inside of us: new perspectives, new understanding and awareness that lead to new outcomes and life direction. But here's the thing, you don't have to be a world traveler to be a "Traveler." We are all on a cosmic journey, traveling through our own life and time, as our souls are ever growing and learning more about who we are and what we want. Lou RichElle Andrade said, "To be a successful traveler means letting go of expectations, trusting the journey and letting love lead. It isn't an outward journey at all, but 100 percent on the inside."

When we change, our dreams will, too.

Before I left for my trip around the world, I made a promise to myself. If you recall, the foundation for the Joy Seeker way of life is:

- Let go of all expectations and be fully in the journey.
- Trust ourselves and life more fully and live openly from our heart.
- See our life as a creative adventure.

And in returning to these guiding principles, I could see how the most important thing was to honor my joy. At that point in my journey, about six months of traveling, I was ready to return to the States for radical reset. Never in a million years did I think my Joy Seeker Journey, the dream to travel for 365 days straight, would result in me returning home halfway through, but that is what my soul needed. This was being true to myself. And I trusted myself enough to know this was the best choice for me. I pursued the dream, I got what I needed. The same situation that once felt good had possibly expired because I learned what I set out to learn. My soul had grown to the next level. The lessons I sought to understand had been addressed. Of course we don't always realize this is happening when we are in it, but reflecting back we can see this is the path for us all. If you are in a situation that once felt great, but the joy is gone, it's often because your soul has grown and you are ready for the next chapter of your life.

So is it time for you to jump ship and head to the next big thing? The real question to ask yourself is, Have you learned what you needed to? If we jump ship and leave the dream without learning the lessons we need to learn, we will find ourselves in the same situation again and again. This is why we leave bad jobs, only to be sitting at a different desk in a different company a few months later feeling the exact same way. The same thing happens with relationships. We leave the dud in search of our stud, only to find ourselves feeling unheard, unseen, and unloved—different place, different face, but same sadness within. We can leave our dreams and trade up for new ones, but when we fail to look at the lessons, and we aren't complete within ourselves, we will always get the same outcome in a different experience. So to make sure we don't repeat the frustrating situations, we learn the lessons. Ask yourself, "Do I feel complete? Have I learned what I needed to from this experience?"

Before leaving a dream that doesn't feel as good as we hoped, we need to be aware of the lessons trying to present themselves. When I wrote my book *Adventures for Your Soul*, I moved to Hawaii for three months with the goal to move there full-time. My outcome, the breakthrough I wanted, was to be an island girl. But when I went and wrote my book, challenges came up. Huge challenges that actually made it difficult to write portions of the book and run my coaching business. When I was in Kauai, it was common for the power on part of the island to go out (the part I was on of course). I would be on a coaching call and suddenly the internet dropped, or I would be in the middle of uploading a video to YouTube and everything would disappear. That and the tsunami warnings made it hard for me to focus. At first, I was furious because the reality of living on a tropical island was not matching the dream I had in my head. But then I shifted my anger to appreciation. As Tony Robbins says, "You can't be angry and grateful at the same time." What I needed to do was take stock and look at my circumstances without emotion. I removed my frustration and looked at the pros and cons of living on an island. I had been there for three months and the final month of working was very painful for me. Nothing was working, so everything took extra-long to do. I didn't know it at the time but there were lessons presenting themselves to me. When nothing was flowing in Hawaii, and I kept holding on and digging my feet in to try to make it work and prove to myself and others that I could make it work, the Universe was actually teaching me a valuable lesson: It's okay to change course. In retrospect, I should have recognized that that dream had an expiration date and I stayed past it. I had learned everything I needed and could have left early to finish my book in a place that brought me more joy, but I hunkered down and pushed through. (Which is why, in my Joy Seeker Journey traveling the world, it was much easier to recognize the signs from the Universe and be okay with changing course. I had learned we never have to stay in situations that don't make us feel good.)

We often do this: We roll up our sleeves and fight against what is not working. The most important thing is your joy. It is essential you focus on feeling it. If you aren't happy or feeling connected to your experiences, then it's time to reevaluate. In this part of your journey, don't be afraid to change course or at least consider what else could be. If you hold on like I did in Hawaii, you actually waste time and energy in your precious life and most importantly, you aren't honoring yourself.

There is absolutely nothing wrong with being true to yourself, which sometimes means changing course. Our ego mind tries to tell us it is failure or we are weak, but your true self knows that it is really just honoring the rhythms of your true self. Changing your mind is actually transformation in action. When we feel the inner nudge to try something new or leave a situation that no longer brings us joy or feels good, we are giving ourselves an opportunity to grow. Especially if you feel trapped, controlled, manipulated, or worried for your well-being, it is essential you leave the situation. Look at your life like chapters of a book. Each chapter is a choice that connects to the next chapter, and although together they create the full beautiful story, each chapter as it is unfolding is the most important thing. When you make choices, instead of thinking, *This is my end-all, be-all choice*, simply say, "This is the next chapter. And I am making the choice that feels the best based on what feels good right now."

Instead of pushing through and forcing things to flow, ask yourself, "What is the lesson I am learning right now?" For me the lesson was to learn how to not push and I never

Sometimes the best follow-through is to surrender fully.

have to stay in any situation that doesn't make me feel good. I may have not learned the lesson when in Hawaii, but I promised myself to never do that again, to never stay in a situation that is painful just to prove I can do it.

Staying in a dream past its expiration date not only hurts you, but it hurts your future self because you are preventing yourself from reaching fulfillment and happiness. While traveling the world full-time for a year, I thought about that promise I made to myself several years back and the Universe gave me an opportunity to apply the lesson. I allowed my Hawaiian dream to transform me. I've grown into a more authentic version of myself who has new priorities, new hopes, and new dreams. I got to live that big dream. I have seen it through to its natural completion. Although it isn't necessarily what I thought it would be (a full year abroad), it is 100 percent what it needed to be. Perhaps the most significant shift was, I no longer needed to see the world in order to feel like I belonged in the world. So I booked my next flight, not to some exotic location or new destination, but back home, to Portland, Oregon. My goal of traveling for 365 days straight had expired after six months because I gave myself full permission to do what feels right, to always honor my heart's pull and be true to myself.

Joy Jaunt: Allow the Unfolding

We feel resistance and stress when we are attached to outcome. The main problem is our expectations. When we can release expectation and surrender ourselves fully to the experience, we will feel more ease. Ask yourself:

• What expectation has been holding me back?

- Where have I been focusing on how it is supposed to look?
- Where have I been pretending things are better than they actually are?

Then gently go inward and release the resistance by trusting the journey and the unfolding.

- What is opening up for me?
- What would bring me more joy?

Radical Recap

Changing your mind or leaving a situation is not bad as long as you are following your heart and listening to your inner voice. Sometimes we outgrow what we once needed to grow into. When you experience new things, you grow.

AWESOME OPPORTUNITY: Let yourself grow by letting go of the old and opening up to the new.

MANTRA: "I trust the unfolding and allow myself to grow."

Your Future Self
Is Waiting

—

TRUST YOURSELF

*There are some things one can only achieve by a
deliberate leap in the opposite direction.*

—Franz Kafka

O NCE YOU RELEASE RESISTANCE AND allow the unfolding of your life, your true self will emerge and you will
feel more balanced and peaceful than you ever have. But
this release does not necessarily come easy. Old habits and
false beliefs keep us tied to dreams that no longer serve us.
One of the false beliefs we carry with us is guilt. We feel
guilty when we let go, like maybe we will make a mistake,
or we are to blame for it not working. We think if maybe we
tried harder, worked more, done something different, then
the outcome would have been different, but this is simply
our fear mind. As long as you showed up fully and did everything you could, you did enough. And your enough is
always enough.

As long as we are focusing on what went wrong or how things feel different from what we thought, we can't see what is going right. If you find yourself in a situation you recently let go of, instead of focusing on how it didn't work out, turn your attention to what you want now. Align with feeling good. And consider it actually did work out because you got what you needed. Accept that the dream has expired, so now what? Whether it's a divorce, a breakup, a career change, or ending a trip early, letting go is grace in action.

We have to be willing to let go of what's no longer working in order to create space for the new to come in.

Of course there are some pieces of our life that are absolutely worth fighting for, especially when they involve other people, so you need to be really honest with yourself and ask if it is worth it. But at a soul level, in your heart of hearts, you know when it's right, when it's worth that fight, when throwing in the towel isn't an option. The first few months of me traveling the world full-time there were many difficult moments, but I never once thought about ending the trip until I got to a point where I felt like not ending my trip would cause regret.

Joy Jaunt: Reevaluate Your Life

So how do we truly know when it is time to reevaluate our life? We turn inward and get honest. Free write and answer these key questions.

Ask yourself:

- How does this situation make me feel?
- How do I want to feel?
- What is most important to me right now?
- Who have I become in pursuing this goal/dream?
- Has this chapter, dream expired?
- What can I let go of that no longer brings me joy?
- Do I feel complete?
- What new insights, opportunities, ideas are coming to me?
- Let the answers you uncover inspire you and help move you forward.

———————————

Recognize that the Universe is giving you clarity for the next steps for your life. You are clearer about what you want to do and who you want to be. It is now about having the courage to do it.

Before making my choice to end my travel around the world, I asked myself these questions below. The answers confirmed that it was the right time to end a dream and go home to start the next chapter of my life.

Top Signs It Is Time to Let Go and Move On

☐ Do my thoughts go to memories more than the present?
☐ Does the situation cause more pain than joy?

☐ Am I hoping and pleading for the person, place, or situation to change?

☐ Have I become complacent, bored, or resentful?

☐ Is the pattern persisting even though I tried to fix it?

☐ Do I feel alone, unheard, or disrespected?

☐ Is this situation holding me back from growing and being who I want to be?

☐ Am I hoping and expecting things to get better?

☐ Do I cry more than I laugh?

☐ Do I feel exhausted emotionally, spiritually, and physically?

☐ Have I lost my passion and joy?

☐ Am I sacrificing who I really am?

☐ Have I stopped having fun? Have I stopped dreaming?

☐ Am I holding on because of fear of the unknown?

This list serves as a compassionate guide to help you make the right choice for *you*. If you found yourself saying yes to the majority of these questions, consider it may be time for you to take a step forward and let go. Trust your future and know you will be guided to happiness. Your higher self is giving you support, so lean into this as you move forward. Know that you are not off track at all, and the more you give yourself permission to re-lease what is no longer working, the sooner you can meet the happy, healthy, joy-filled you. Your future self is waiting.

Life is a balance of holding on and letting go.

Radical Recap

Changing your mind is not a sign you are off track. Your future self is always guiding you.

AWESOME OPPORTUNITY: Pay attention to your inner voice and the inspiration that comes from within; it is supporting you. Start to trust it and act on its guidance.

MANTRA: "My life is an adventure; I enjoy the new beginnings."

Accept the Invitation to Grow

TRUST THE PROCESS

We must be willing to let go of the life we have planned, so as to have the life that is waiting for us.

—E. M. FORSTER

ONE OF THE BEST WAYS to know when it is time to move on is when you have stopped growing. My good friend Mel Wells, the bestselling author of *The Goddess Revolution* and founder of The Self-Love Summit in the United Kingdom, is an excellent example of accepting the invitation to grow. A few years ago, she moved to Bali, Indonesia, and when I was traveling in 2016 we met up at a café on the island. As we sat over brunch and green juice, we shared our goals. I asked her what was next, and she said she loved Bali and planned on staying as long as she could because it made her happy. Flash-forward two years when she made a huge announcement that she would be moving back to London.

When I spoke to her about her choice, she told me, "I love Bali. It was home when I needed it. I mean why on earth would I move back to London? It's cold, and expensive and stressful, but you know what? It was time. It was time to leave the island, because I was too comfortable. I wasn't

Let yourself grow by letting go.

growing." And there it was, the truth to what we all need and understand: Growth is the core of joy. And today she is happy living in London leading sold-out retreats and summits all while living her passion. She wasn't afraid to change course, and she certainly didn't care or worry about what others thought about her choice, because she knew the decision was for her and her own soul's growth. Although moving to Bali was a huge dream of hers, it expired, and she had to let herself grow by letting go.

Joy Jaunt: Rewrite Your Story

Answering these questions is key to helping you get to the core of what you really want for your life at this next phase. Remember you are the creator of your own life experience. If something doesn't feel good anymore, it is completely in your control to change directions.

Where have I stopped growing?
What dream am I holding on to that no longer feels good?

What experience have I outgrown?

What's required for a graceful transition is faith and courage. Taking steps forward will be easier when you invite your true self along with you. The reason it was easy for my friend Mel to make such a difficult decision is because she was 100 percent aligned with her true self. She knows what she needs and honors the rhythm of her life. She doesn't see things set in stone; her life is an ever-evolving, unfolding story. Often things we once valued strip away and the core, the truth of us is revealed. It's not a bad thing to change directions. Your life is too short to stay in any situation that prevents your soul from growing.

It's much easier to make a change when you know you are being guided. And when you are connected to your true self, the Universe is with you, giving you support to step gracefully into the real you. Be willing to let go, strip away and release anything and everything that no longer works.

Following through on your dreams takes courage; however, leaving the dream that is no longer working takes even more courage. But when you trust yourself and the Universe, your higher power, it becomes easier.

The entire Joy Seeker Journey is really a dedication to you. By putting yourself in this program, you are really showing up for yourself in profound ways. As you do this, you begin to see how manageable life really can be. You see that the difficulties only come from resistance and when we make choices from a place of love, we are aligned with our true self, and everything is better. You soon see you are not giving up or quitting anything. When you let go of a situation that doesn't work anymore, you are actually being loving to yourself and all those involved. Instead of seeing it as giving up or quitting, realize it is completion. You have arrived in a place where the lessons you needed to learn have been learned, and there is nothing more for you in this stage. It's time now to spread your beautiful gorgeous wings. It's time for you to step into the next best thing for you and fly.

Radical Recap

Giving up is not quitting but actually a sign of completion. You can honor your past by moving forward, this is all part of the growth cycle.

AWESOME OPPORTUNITY: Practice letting go and releasing what no longer works and move forward with confidence that something better is on its way to you.

MANTRA: "There is no such thing as mistakes, it's all growth."

Joy Seeker Journal Time

1. In your workbook or joy journal, take a moment to answer these questions before progressing to the next section
2. Where have I stopped growing?
3. What promise can I make to myself based on past lessons learned?
4. What is most important to me?

— Stay —

IN YOUR

Heart

it will transform

Everything

#JoySeeker

PART 8

THE BEING

How to Be Happy with
Your Extraordinary,
Somewhat Ordinary Life

Challenge Yourself to Go Beyond Your Fears

—

BE WHO YOU'RE MEANT TO BE

All life is an experiment. The more experiments you make the better.

—Ralph Waldo Emerson

WHEN YOU START LIVING YOUR life from a place of power, your time will expand. You will fill up your moments with joy, wonder, and awe and you will feel life more deeply. In this experience, you will see that everything in life is always undone meaning everything is always unfolding, and nothing is ever fully complete. I used to have checklists and to-do sheets. Each day I would check off the boxes, proving I was productive and on track. But every single day there was always more to add. Then it occurred to me that it is always undone. There will always be more to create and do. There will be things left unfinished. This is part of a rich, glorious, depth-filled life.

Before going on my own Joy Seeker Journey, I had a very full schedule. I was maxed out; my every moment was planned. I had to actually schedule in fun. I would write "cuddle time with my dog" or "nature walk" on my to-do list. Seems crazy but so many of us do this. We don't know how to relax or truly have fun. We don't know how to be. We are so busy checking off our lists that we forgot to leave room for the unimaginable.

So often in life we want closure or completion, but life's gift to us is the unfolding experience. The constant changes and new opportunities are part of living an abundant life. Now, instead of trying to complete things and check my to-dos off, I simply see life as an experiment. I still use to-do lists, but I'm no longer so strict about having the list control my day. My worth is no longer tied to how much I get done.

Instead of making a to-do list, I encourage you to make an "I Dare" list. We often learn best when we challenge ourselves. What challenge can you give yourself to reach your growth goals?

One of my clients' dreams was to be a motivational speaker to help women find purpose through their pain. The problem was that she was terrified of public speaking. To help confront her fear, she decided to dare herself to do Facebook Live sessions every day for an entire week. In putting it in terms of a challenge, she was able to push herself outside of her comfort zone and was able to grow into her dream of being a better speaker. What challenge can you give yourself?

I have another client who dreamed of leading retreats for women, but she was terribly shy talking to strangers. I encouraged her to dare herself to go beyond her comfort zone. She decided to challenge herself to start a podcast, and after a year of interviewing people all over the world for her podcast, her show became one of iTunes most popular wellness podcasts, which soon landed her a book deal with her dream publisher and led to an annual retreat. It all started with a challenge she gave herself to be more confident speaking to strangers.

The journey is where we get to try things out. Explore your desires by making fun challenges for yourself, and dive into the journey, your life, with arms wide open. It's all an experiment, so have fun. So many of us are too focused on completion. We look at past relationships that didn't pan out, jobs we left, or situations that ended differently than anticipated and we feel like failures. When we don't have completion, part of us feels incomplete. But this is a fear-based trick. Because the world is always in constant movement, which means things are always going forward, completion is an illusion that separates us from connecting with ourselves and each other. Instead of needing completion, can you focus on what is opening up for you instead?

Joy Jaunt: Dare Yourself to Grow

This exercise will help you move beyond your fear-imposed limitations and make life a glorious experiment.

Put aside your to-do list and instead think about the heart dreams you wish to accomplish. With these dreams in mind, ask yourself the following questions:

1. What is the dream you want to fulfill?
2. What fears are holding you back from moving forward with this dream?

3. What one thing can you do today to move beyond that fear? What can you dare yourself to do?

Challenge yourself to take that first step out of your fear and into your dream.

Radical Recap

In order to get what you want you have to move through your comfort zone.

When you challenge yourself to do new things and experiment with life, you grow. And when you grow you reach your goals more easily.

AWESOME OPPORTUNITY: Dare yourself to do what you are afraid of. Get out of your comfort zone and try something new.

MANTRA: "My life is a daring adventure, one I explore with grace and ease."

Let The Universe Surprise You

———

BE IN THE MOMENT

Look forward to life with wonder, it's all a creative adventure.

—JAMES MARTIN PEEBLES

WE'VE BEEN ON THIS JOY Seeker Journey together for a while now, and I hope you are starting to realize that this isn't a journey to somewhere. Joy isn't something you chase after. It's right where you are. It's a way of experiencing life. When we stop racing to the next best thing, when we stop chasing the shiny new feeling, we can see that joy is right here, right now and find true inner peace. Slowing down and enjoying the journey is the biggest part of the Joy Seeker way of life.

I found true inner peace came with my full surrender. I arrived at a place of being, one with myself and present in the moment, and in this space, the Universe can surprise you. It is a complete spiritual surrender. A release of all ideas you have for yourself because you know the Universe has a plan so much better than yours. This is the time when we co-create with the Universe in a meaningful way. It's when we let the Universe surprise us. The Universe knows what you want and need more than you do because the Universe is you; you are one with it. Your higher self is connected to the source energy, and tapping into your true self is the best way to feel more connected to yourself, your life, and the world. When you are connected to this source energy, you can look forward to life with wonder.

In order to truly surrender, I developed a pattern of detachment. I let go of all expectations and instead trusted the process. And living this way allowed me to live fully in the moment, fully in my joy. I allowed joy to lead me, and my joy opened me up to new possibilities. This way of living opened up extraordinary doors for me.

While I was traveling, I found that my true joy was in connection, family, and intimacy. I also realized that I needed purpose. Living in my joy meant taking my deep desire for connection, purpose, and belonging and combining it with my passion for travel. What my original trip around the world was missing was purpose. By understanding this, I could rewrite my story and devolve a new plan, which led me to become extremely involved with Golden Bond Rescue, a golden retriever rescue organization based in Oregon. I volunteered to fly to China to help rescue dogs in desperate need for good homes. This led me to want to adopt a dog, and now I have a new best friend named Chance, who brings me joy beyond compare. After resetting and realigning with my true self, my Joy Seeker Journey continued, only this time with a focus and clear plan: to help save dogs. My passion now had a purpose.

When I released my expectations, I allowed joy to lead the way and my life blossomed. I was inspired to use my money and time to volunteer with organizations I cared about.

When you live with complete faith, you trust in yourself deeply and life will move you forward with ease and grace. Your full surrender will be rewarded.

Allow your true self to be seen and heard in ways you never have before by surrendering to the present moment. The next level you has arrived. This is the real you. Ask yourself, "Now that I have become who I want to be, what does this person need? How can I honor who I am at this phase of my life?" And embrace the answers with enthusiasm, reveling in the freedom to be you.

This time in our life feels so good because our needs are being met, because we're making choices that allow us to be fully actualized. New awareness, new goals, new dreams, new desires will be birthed into existence.

Let yourself play with the world and connect to your own purpose and passion; let it lead you. What new venture, idea, creative impulse or is coming to you? Explore it.

Joy is now rooted deep inside your heart. It is no longer outside of you; it is you. Joy is about living as fully as possible

The joy is in the journey.

in the moment. It's not about how many to-dos you check off your list. It has nothing to do with how packed we fill our life. It is about how deep we go. Allow yourself to feel all of life, and be in the moment for whatever the moment contains.

It can be scary to go for something new after changing course, because it is unfamiliar, but that is the exciting part. When it feels intimidating, it is growth. And just like that

When you understand that everything is working for you and never against you, you begin to be extraordinarily connected and able to decipher what brings you great joy.

your current self is your authentic self. This part of you has been here all along; there were just fears, insecurities, and limiting beliefs blocking you. You see, you aren't becoming anything you aren't already, but rather you are allowing yourself to be who you truly are, and who we are is always growing, changing, and revealing. This is when we emerge, open up, and discover who we are meant to be. Let your life excite you.

When we stop trying to plan out everything and control every outcome, we can co-create with the Universe and open up to our deepest desires from a heart-centered place.

Joy Jaunt: What's Next? Open Up to the New

What are you curious about? What are your passions?

Now that you are living the dreams you set out to live, commit yourself to more growth.

What new direction are you ready to go in?

If you weren't doing what you currently are doing, what would you want to be doing?

What is next?

Radical Recap

When you let go of trying to control the outcome and surrender to your life experience, joy can guide you and provide you with unlimited fulfillment.

AWESOME OPPORTUNITY: Stop resisting the changes that are emerging and embrace the unknown. Let go so you can grow.

MANTRA: "Joy is my guide; I trust it fully."

Stay In Your Heart: It Will Transform Everything

—

BE IN YOUR HEART

Your heart knows what your head has yet to figure out. Trust it.

—Shannon Kaiser

There will be times in your life when all your instincts will tell you to do something that defies logic, upsets your plans, and may seem crazy to others. When this happens, do not back down. Now is not the time to shy away. Go for it. Listen to your instincts, trust yourself; your true self is talking to you. Go ahead and ignore everything else because this is the path of the true you. It doesn't matter what you said you would do, or the route you were on. What matters is that you trust this instinct and go forth from the place you are right now. This is the way of the heart.

Living from your heart takes courage. It takes a blind faith and unshakable trust, but once you tap into this lifestyle, you can never go back because it feels so good. For the first time in your life, it feels right. Your heart is your compass. It has insights, guidance, and wisdom that your head just can't understand.

I made a commitment to myself to always follow my heart, which meant turning my back on logic many times. This is how I lead my life and it has never led me astray. But I understand this way of living is confusing and scary for many. When I first left my corporate job, I moved back home and lived in my parents' basement for a summer. I took a minimum wage job at a clothing store and just tried to get clear about what I wanted to do for a living.

Your head is the ana- lytical, ego part of you. It is where fear lives. But your heart is love, joy, and knowing. Your heart is trusting and believing. Your heart is your compass.

(This was before I discovered my passion for writing and pursued my life coaching practice.) I wasn't sure which direction I wanted to follow, but I did decide that I wanted a new car, my dream car, a new Jeep Wrangler. My boyfriend at the time had an incredibly hard time understanding this. At dinner with my family one night, he argued with me and said, "You want to buy a brand-new car but you're only making minimum wage, you live in your parents' basement, and you don't even know what you want to do for a living. That makes no sense at all." Then my dad chimed in and said, "You need to understand that this is the way Shannon is. She makes choices that don't make much sense to others. They even defy logic. But it always works out for her. You just have to trust her that she knows what she wants and needs and is doing what's right for her." And this is how I always try to lead my life, from a place of deep trust and knowing, making all choices from my heart. I trust things will work out because they always do. I ended up getting that brand-new $23,000 car, and not only did I pay it off, but also built a thriving life coaching and speaking career on top of it because I trusted and led with faith. I let my heart lead; I let love lead. And today I am still driving my red Jeep. It's a wonderful reminder of what's possible when you believe in yourself and your dreams.

When you trust and have faith, everything is possible. Tap into the love. Love is your highest self, your soul self. Love knows you better than you know you. Tap into that energy of knowing and believe in the power of yourself and your goals. Your heart center is a direct connection to source energy, the divine light. Today, I make all choices from this heart-centered place. It may not make sense to others, but that doesn't matter. When you make choices from your heart, it has nothing to do with anyone else because it is your soul's journey. It is your own highest good in action.

Being true to ourselves is so much easier when we are supporting ourselves emotionally, physically, and spiritually. The best way to support yourself is to trust your heart and lean into its guidance. What is your heart telling you? What message does it have for you?

The missing ingredient for so many of us is faith. Faith is believing in what you can't see. It is trusting in the unknown and believing in the process. Allow yourself to be more in the journey and let go of the outcome. This is faith moving through you. Give yourself permission to trust, because in the space of faith, you will step into a life beyond your wildest dreams.

Radical Recap

When you support yourself it's easier for your dreams to come true.

Your dreams are for you, believe in them and trust them; when you do you live a miraculous life.

AWESOME OPPORTUNITY: Your heart is guiding you, so trust it.

MANTRA: "I believe in myself. My heart knows what is best for me; I trust it."

R.S.V.P to the Dance

—

BE PRESENT

What lies behind you and what lies in front of you, pales in comparison to what lies inside of you.

—RALPH WALDO EMERSON

WHAT A JOURNEY IT IS to be alive! When we let joy be our compass, it is a magnificent creative adventure where you get to explore the myriad layers of yourself. I like to think of life as a dance and you have an invitation to this grand party. But how much you dance is up to you. It is always your choice. You can take to the floor or sit on the sidelines. But even if you don't show up at all, the dance will continue. Life is always in motion, things are always unfolding, and you can move with the changes or resist.

What you will soon see is that every single part of life is precious because you are living from intention and love. As you do this your world becomes lighter, more carefree, and

294

peaceful. The things that used to bother you have fallen far away. You are happier and healthier than you've ever been, and it is because you are showing up on the dance floor that is your life. You will arrive at this phase when you have surrendered fully into your own life and accepted the invitation to the dance that is life. You will have no expectations attached to the outcome or arriving at one specific spot on the dance floor, for the movement is the experience. Moving in your life, making choices, aligning yourself with love is the ultimate dance. In this dance, your partner is the Universe, God, source energy, love. When you step onto the dance floor, love will lead you, and you will see that everything is in perfect order. There is nothing to force or fix or change. Everything is as it should be. You can relax into the rhythm and enjoy the movement. This is a time in your life where clarity is your constant. You will be edging into enlightenment. It is love expressed through you. You see and feel heaven on earth.

When you start to live in this new manner, where light is your compass and you trust your intuition and the unbiased love of the Universe, there is an undeniable peace in your heart. You accept all that is and graciously open yourself up to each moment, for you know that is all we truly have. There are many ways to be more present in your life; the fastest way is to drop from your head into your heart. Being present is powerful, for it gives you an unmatchable sense of joy. And what is happening in that moment isn't what brings you joy; you are the expression of joy in its entirety. You could be exploring a new country and eating foreign food that enlightens your senses, or you could be wrapped up in an excellent read on your couch at home. The joy will be the same for you have mastered the art of being present. You have mastered the art of being you.

Joy isn't something you chase. It's something you express. Now that you've arrived at the stage, the grand glorious dance floor, you get to dance. This means you get to express yourself fully. It is all about you, darling, and your effortless way of being your unique, beautiful, magnificent self. The more present you are on the dance floor of your life, the easier your life will be. Instead of judging situations or trying to change them, you let them be. You don't try to change the dance. You just simply be in it. You are one with it.

What you do or where you go has nothing to do with your capacity to be in joy, for it is in you always.

Being present for the dance of your life doesn't mean you avoid hardship and pain, but it does mean you feel less hardship and pain. Because in your new awareness, with the love source energy flowing through you, and your connection to your divine true self, you now know you are always being provided for. Your higher power and true self are not going to give you anything you can't truly handle. In trusting the Universe so fully, you lean forward into your life with a great big effortless leap. The things that used to scare you are now just an illusion that's been shattered. The unknown, fear of what people think, all of it is behind you. For you are living 100 percent in accordance with you.

We get to this place when we stop trying to get to this place. We stop racing through our life and let ourselves be. Instead of doing more to reach joy, you be more of you. Once you grasp this, you see life is quite simple. It's the pushing against what is that restricts us. This journey has profound gifts for you. Each moment of your life is like a treasure waiting to be discovered. It's wonderful to have goals and dreams. We can let them guide us forward. *But* the real magic of our life, the true inspiration and joy, comes with us being our true self, and that is not dependent on anything outside of you.

Instead of needing a specific goal to come true for you to be happy, simply go even bigger and have a goal that you trust the Universe, and yourself more fully. Have the goal that you are always right where you need to be with the people you need to be with. This will guide your life in miraculous ways. Release the need to control anything, and your trust in everything will gracefully move you forward.

Our life is a dance, and we all should be dancing our hearts out with joy. The more we live with presence and self-awareness, the more rewarding the dance. But it isn't about how grand or big your life is. It's about the dance steps and the exploration. Each and every move is the unfolding. It's the pure joy of the moment. The more movement you try, the more you explore, the more you move with the feelings within you, the more joyful your life will be. The more connected you feel, the more love you'll experience. For you will be living your life from a place of authenticity. The dance is happening whether you participate or not, will you accept your invitation?

Radical Recap

Life is a dance and you are invited to the dance floor.
Pure joy is in the moment and each step you take.

AWESOME OPPORTUNITY: Show up for the dance.

MANTRA: "I am the creator of my own masterful dance. I show up for all of life's experiences."

Things Aren't Always What They Seem

BE AWARE OF THE BEAUTY

*You are the Universe, expressing itself as a
human for a little while.*

—ECKHART TOLLE

BEFORE I DECIDED TO TRAVEL the world, I was living in a rented condo. I remember about a week before I moved out, after living there for two whole years, I saw the most beautiful view of Mount Hood. Mount Hood is a famous mountain in Oregon and can be seen from different places around the Portland metropolitan area. That day, as I was driving down my street, getting ready to turn into my driveway, I looked up and what I saw took my breath away. The sun was setting and hitting the mountain in such a way that I was awestruck. My first thought was, *Oh my gosh how gorgeous!* That thought was immediately followed up by, *What? Wait. I've never seen that mountain there before. Has that always been there? I've lived here for two years and have never seen it.* It occurred to me that beauty is all around us all the time, but most of the time we can't see it. Our vision is blocked by our own expectations, judgments, and fears. We are too focused on our own dramas and life demands. Here was one of the most beautiful natural scenes I ever witnessed right outside my door and I had never seen it before. I made myself a promise right then and there to take the blinders off. By becoming conscious of my surroundings, by making an effort to look around, I gained more appreciation for life and the moment and was able to see things that were always there with a fresh set of eyes. The environment was the same, but I shifted my own perception and now I could see it.

Looking for beauty in all things is a gift to yourself and the world.

This moment was a gift because I could finally see what I had been missing for so long: the present moment. The present moment is all that we have. It is the only guarantee in our life. The more present we can be, the more we will see that we are one with everything on the planet. We are all children of love, God, the Universe. We are connected to everything around us. Seeing the beauty that is all around is a gift you can give to yourself. When you pause and see life as an unfolding process instead of a race you need to complete, you can relax, release, and surrender even more fully to the journey. It's a beautiful ride when you coast instead of slam your pedal to the metal. When you are fully present in your life, you are full of love, and because of this you will see grand beauty and opportunities everywhere.

In seeing what is and accepting all, you can see the divine light in everything. You experience the magic of living and begin to feel more connected to everything. When I saw that mountain, the most picturesque view, I realized heaven is on earth. I was witnessing it.

We are living in a wonderland, if we slow down and let ourselves see.

Radical Recap

Beauty is all around us; we just need to slow down and be present to see.

AWESOME OPPORTUNITY: Looking for beauty in everything is a gift to yourself and the world.

MANTRA: "I see awe and wonder in everything."

Chance It

—

BE WILLING TO TAKE RISKS

*Let your alignment (with Well-Being) be first
and foremost, and let everything else be
secondary. And not only will you have an
eternally joyous journey, but everything you
have ever imagined will flow effortlessly into
your experience. There is nothing you cannot be
or do or have.*

—ESTHER HICKS

IN DEDICATING AN ENTIRE YEAR to pursuing joy and
seeking out more connection and purpose, I discovered
a new way of being. The secret? It's really just *trusting* life
and taking more chances.

How do we do this?

We trust ourselves more.

If we are honest with ourselves, our feelings are always
trying to show us the way—you will know the right path by

how you feel. Does the choice make you feel expansive, joy-ful, hopeful, and optimistic? Or does it make you feel trapped, concerned, worried, or fearful? The answers are already within us. We never have to struggle or second-guess our-selves again. I see it all the time with life coaching clients, friends, and even in my own life. We get an inkling, a gut feel-ing, an intuitive nudge that clearly aligns us with our highest good, yet we overanalyze, question, and second-guess it. We don't follow through because we worry it could be the wrong choice. But the more we listen to this intuition—the feelings that say go for it, trust yourself, it will work out—the easier everything will be. If we just listen to that inner voice, the one that knows us best, then we will live a peaceful, abun-dant, fulfilled life.

I decided to try this process out, by leaning into life and trusting the unknown more. It looked like this . . .

As I mentioned, once I ended my worldwide traveling and returned to Portland, Oregon, I became heavily involved with a rescue dog organization called Golden Bond Rescue, donat-ing my time, energy, and resources to help save golden retrievers and try to find them good homes. I told myself it was a way to honor Tucker, my dog who passed, and who originally inspired the entire Joy Seeker Journey. Because I was so connected to who I really am and was in alignment with my values and true self, I knew I wanted to travel with a purpose, which is what was missing previously in the year. I escorted the dogs from China back to the States. I remem-ber being on the airplane, flying over the Pacific Ocean with seven dogs in crates, feeling a sense of connection, joy, love, and purpose. I knew this is what it's all about. Aligning with my true self, deliberately moving through each day with purpose, inspired by peace and joy. This was the path to lasting happiness. This was enlightenment.

When we make choices from this place of alignment, we take more chances. Not from a place of fear or risk, but rather a place of joy. When you are aligned with your true self, your choices become easier. You know without a doubt what is most important to you and you make choices from this place of power.

My connection to these dogs was so strong, the one I adopted, I named Chance, because not only was I giving

The only sustainable form of long-term happiness is to be in alignment with our authentic self.

him a second chance at life, rescuing him from China, but he was also my second chance at furry love. But most importantly, what the word *chance* represents is taking a leap of faith. Not knowing the outcome, but trusting so deeply within yourself, that everything will fall into place.

We have to take more chances in life. We have to try more experiences and go for what we truly want. We have to be willing to go on epic journeys, to stand up for what we believe in. You owe it to yourself to go after your own happiness. The key to all of our peace and joy is in taking more chances. I took a chance coming back to Portland early, which led to me getting more involved with the dog recue, which led to another adventure overseas, which led to me adopting Chance, the new love of my life. This beautiful unfolding happened because I trusted joy and made choices from my heart. When I first offered to volunteer with the organization, I didn't know it would lead me to meet the new love of my life.

I just knew I needed to listen to that inner voice that said, "Yes, this feels good. This feels right."

When we trust ourselves, the Universe delivers every time. We can walk courageously into the unknown because we know that we are being guided. When you live your life with this faith and unbiased trust in yourself and the Universe, you cannot be off track or make a mistake, because you are being who you are meant to be. You are living the life you were made for.

Always go in the direction of what feels good even if it doesn't make sense. It is always for your highest good.

When you are in tune with who you really are and what is most important to you, your choices become so much easier. You are guided from within, and you know *you cannot make a mistake.*

Instead of leaning into fear, let's lean into faith. Let's listen to our inner voice, the one that says *keep going, follow your heart, trust the process.* Your inner guide is your best tool for a happy life. And it's been trying to guide you this entire time. Your feelings that keep popping up, they're all part of your bigger plan. All you have to do is stop resisting, and trust life a little more. Take the chance, go for it. We are never the same once we step forward into the unknown and push past our fears, once we say yes to life and choose joy as our compass. When you commit to your dreams and live from your heart, you can't go back to the way you used to be. And that's a beautiful thing because all of it leads you to everything you are supposed to be. Don't resist your life; dive in fully and embrace all that is emerging.

Radical Recap

When we trust ourselves, the Universe delivers every time.

AWESOME OPPORTUNITY: Take more chances and explore life; fulfillment lives in the unknown.

MANTRA: "I take more chances and enjoy life's journey."

Your Truth

——

BE THE LIGHT

We are a way for the Universe to know itself.
Some part of our being knows this is where we
came from. We long to return. And we can, be-
cause the cosmos is also within us. We're made
of star stuff.

—CARL SAGAN

E MAY THINK WE KNOW what we want, but rest as-
sured the Universe always knows what is truly best
for us. When I say the Universe, really, I am referencing
source love, the energy of divinity and your higher self. It is
all the same; there is no separation. And this became crystal
clear to me when I returned to Costa Rica to close out my Joy
Seeking year.

Toward the end of my year long dedication to joy, I had
the opportunity to visit Rythmia again, the healing center,
and participate in shamanic journeys. At that point in my life,

I was good. I felt extraordinary happiness, joy, a deep connection to myself, my career, and my life. Why go to a healing center? Because I was called. My soul called me; I felt the pull to go. We all have these pulls, from the heart, from our soul, that say, "This is for your highest good." We must continue to trust and respect these nudges and openly accept the invitation to play with the world. I trusted this guidance and dived in deeply to another travel experience.

With this in mind the shamans asked us to set an intention before the sacred ceremony. And my intention, after traveling and dedicating my year to joy, was to "show me who I will become." I wanted to know the next level of joy. Where was all this leading? Secretly hoping to confirm my desires, I wanted to see visions of me on Ted Talk stages and selling millions of books and becoming a #1 *New York Times* bestseller. Would I see myself leading even more retreats around the world and staying connected to my joy in everything that I do? The intention was enticing. It was intoxicating to think about what I might become. After all, when we do all this work on ourselves, what's next? The sky is the limit, right?

I dived into my shamanic journey with a focus on the future. "Show me who I will become." As the evening turned into early morning, I found myself feeling a little deflated. I still hadn't gotten any clarity or insights about my future. Feeling slightly let down, I surrendered. I decided it wasn't important and I would just participate fully in the journey right now. Which meant, let go of all expectations and just be present for what is unfolding.

And then the shamans called us up for a blessing. We sat in a half circle and for what I wished was an eternity, but was really closer to forty minutes, I got my miracle. As the shamans danced, chanted, sang, and brushed me with leaves, the ritual took hold and love poured through my every fiber. I felt so cared for—seven shamans all focusing on me, tending to me, clearing my energy and loving me, for me. As they worked their magic and focused on the blessing, I ascended into a higher vibration and felt more love than I've ever felt before. My entire body felt like it would burst with loving compassion. All I saw was bright white light and my inner voice said, "*This! This is it!!!* This is who you will become, because this is who you are: *love and light.*"

Tears of joy, of wonder, of gratitude fell from my eyes. It suddenly all made so much sense. I thought my future needed to be some destination I could aspire to, a new accolade, a life achievement benchmark, a goal manifested, but in that moment I saw that none of that really matters. It is not who we are. It is what we are. And what we are is love. We all come from light, for we are light. And the shamans blessed me with the vision of truth, that joy is our truth, and it is all we need for a good life.

Every single one of us is part of the same light, yet so many of us feel and see separation. We think we are separate from everyone else; this pushing against others keeps us from accessing our truth. I knew I needed to stay connected to this truth, because this feeling of pure love felt more joyful than anything I had ever experienced before. It was more joyful than any outer accomplishment. And this feeling was real—it was in me all along.

This light is yours, too. No one can take it from you. No matter what you go through in life, no matter what chapter you are in or what setback comes crashing in, you are eternal light. You are not what you do or where you live or what you have. All that is just part of being alive, and having goals and things that make us feel alive and purposeful is wonderful.

It's part of living a rich life. But defining myself by these goals is what died that day. I no longer need to reach anything in order to be happy or connected to my true self. It doesn't matter what I might become, because I am already all that I can be. You too, you don't have to change yourself or become anything. It's all there inside of you, already beaming within. So let's agree to let go of the trying, and the needing to know our future and the outcome. Let's surrender our life to the greater notion that all is in right order. Because my true self is, just like you are and always will be, enough.

Radical Recap

Nothing exists outside of yourself; it is all within. You are connected to all with your love and light.

AWESOME OPPORTUNITY: Don't be afraid to be seen and show your true self. Be the light that you are.

MANTRA: "I am divine love. I am magnificent light."

Homeward Bound

BE HOME

The Universe is not outside of you. Look inside yourself;
everything that you want, you already are.

—RUMI

ALTHOUGH I DIDN'T KNOW IT at the time, I set out to travel the world for an entire year because I was looking for something I had yet to find. I spent decades always feeling like I didn't fit in. But for me, it was always a race to the next level, searching for meaning in the things that I did or the places I went. I was chasing a feeling outside of myself. I needed to feel something I had yet to find, and I was certain I would feel it with the next place, the next big rush, and the next anything. It wasn't until I dived so fully into my life and participated in my own Joy Seeker Journey that I saw the truth. What I spent years looking for was an illusion, like a mirage in the desert.

I feel as if I've spent my entire life, more than three decades, chasing this dream, to be fulfilled and content with life and my place in it, and the chase was what I was accustomed to. I spent so long looking for it that it became my identity. I was on a quest to find myself, but we can't find what isn't lost. I thought I was missing connection, I felt lost, but the Joy Seeker Journey showed me when we are connected to divine love and our light within, we are never lost, we are never off track, nor are we ever behind. For it's all our life, a magnificent grand quest we actively participate in. You can't mess up an adventure, for the very structure of it is exploration. Once I saw my life as a creative adventure, I could see that the pressure I was putting on myself to find myself, to find my life purpose, to find self-love, to discover lasting joy, was all in itself an illusion keeping me from seeing the truth.

We are what we want.

What I was looking for was home. I wanted to feel at peace, and I believed finding the perfect place on earth would be my golden ticket to endless happy. I traveled to over fifty countries in search of this feeling, and that feeling never showed up in the experiences or the destinations. It just kept eluding me. For years, I kept chasing it, like a carrot on a stick dangling in front of me. I just kept running full speed forward. But this constant chase, running after what you can never reach, is immensely painful. It's exhausting and a lonely way to live. When you fully dive into your life, you will get off the merry-go-round. That chase will no longer be your motivation. Instead you will see that everything you need and want is already here. It's within you.

A couple years ago I was being interviewed for a radio show, and the interviewer asked me, "Who is a person who inspires you?" I thought for a moment and then said,

"Normally I would say someone like Elizabeth Gilbert, the author of *Eat Pray Love*, or Oprah, but honestly, I empower me. I am inspired by me. I've worked hard to be where I am and today I love me." This shocked the radio host at first and she said, "Wow, no one has ever said themselves, and some may think that is egotistical or conceited." But this is not egotistical. When we fully feel self-love and we are actively living an authentic life, being your own hero unapologetically is standard. It's an honor to show up so fully for you. Don't be afraid to be your own hero.

This journey we've been on together, the Joy Seeker way of life, has shown me the real joy in life. It's as if I have been searching endlessly for my golden ticket, the pot of gold at the end of the rainbow. Well, I found it. Never before have I felt so balanced and connected. I am one with myself and the Universe. I have found my treasure chest. Inside is what I've been looking for my entire life. It's not piles of money, the goal weight, the soul mate, fame, achievements, or even success. It's not at all what I thought I was looking for. And it's not what I thought I would find.

The only thing inside this treasure chest is a mirror.

Welcome home.

I have been a
Seeker,
and still am.
But I stopped
asking the books and the stars
I started listening to the
teaching of my
Soul.

-Rumi

The Joy Seeker Way

BE JOY

The Universe is saying: "Allow me to flow through you unrestricted, and you will see the greatest magic you have ever seen."

—Klaus Joehle

WHAT IS A JOY SEEKER? You have signed a sacred contract to show up for yourself, to live from your heart, and be true to yourself in all aspects of your life. When we set out to Joy Seek, we are choosing to live our life on a new level. A level of acceptance, peace and full surrender. Your life is easier, more enjoyable, less dramatic, and more fun. You see how effortless it is to be you and how much joy can be found in even the simplest of things. For it was never about the grand big showcase, but the true nature you bring to each moment. To be a Joy Seeker is to say, *I matter and my life is worth living.* You have arrived in a place where you see that all of your life is a playful adventure, one you get to create and grow and change with. You can release the pressure you put on yourself. Your life is a journey for you and your soul's growth. The people you choose, the places you choose to go, the choices you make—all are part of your adventure. The adventure is yours. If you don't like the story, you can change, you can leave, you can quit, and you can abandon the mission. It's all part of living a life that is fully connected to who you really are.

The Joy Seeker is an approach to life where you choose to be love and make your choices from an aligned place. As you show up more fully in the world, your love and light extend out. You help others access their own truth by just being you. There is no more judgment or shame; there is no more comparison, for you

When you can honor yourself, you honor all those around you.

see you are love in full expression. Love is your compass forward and you feel inner peace that stays with you always. It's peaceful here, it is joyful, and the magic is in every moment. This way of life is not for everyone. Some people need the drama to function, and they want the depths of contrast and the pain that can come with being alive. But not you, my friend, you want more from your life. You don't want to be in pain. Suffering is not the way you choose to live. You no longer attach yourself to anything, for you see detaching from outcomes and expectations is the easiest way to live. There is a graceful, effortless glow that extends from you now; it is a peace that exudes from you. You've transformed. There is a presence within you. Your eyes say it all. They are full of love, warmth, compassion. You are a gift to this world. You see how special our time is, how important this life is,

When peace is your priority, negativity cannot exist.

⌒

and how magnificent it is to be alive. This is the way of the Joy Seeker.

The Joy Seeker way of life is about being 100 percent honest and true to who you are and what you want. This way of life is freeing. It is enriching and extremely satisfying. It is an authentic approach to living your extraordinary life.

Afterword

The Joy Seeker Manifesto

So here we are, at the end of our quest together, but truly it is a brand-new beginning. This experience has allowed us to learn more about our true self so we can live a life with more meaning. A life we feel connected to, a life that feels good on every level. Joy Seeking was never about *the seek*, but the allowing. I admit Joy Allowing makes for an odd book title, but what we learn when we go on our own Joy Seeking mission is that life is not about how big you live, but how deeply you go.

I thought my Joy Seeking mission was about living life as fully as possible and maximizing every moment. Making sure to fill it to the brim. Leave no stone unturned, check everything off the bucket list, explore all possibilities presented. But as I set out to live this type of life, not only was it exhausting, but it felt superficial; it lacked depth. I was missing the meaning and the real connection. Chasing every goal and dream without allowing myself to be present left me overwhelmed and searching for deeper meaning.

Don't get me wrong, it's important to have desires. We can live a life dedicated to our dreams, but the fulfillment doesn't come from our dreams. It comes from the connection we feel as we live our life in pursuit of them. It's about building a strong relationship with self.

It occurred to me that an extraordinary life isn't about how much you do or where you go or even why you do it. Living an extraordinary life is about listening to your heart, being true to yourself, and loving who you are and where you are. When you tap into this way of being, you are one with the Universe. Your life is no longer a conquest but a journey from your own heart. An extraordinary life can be quite ordinary, and that is the magic of it all.

Living a life with meaning comes when we know what is important to us and set up our life to support that.

Living a full life is about growing with yourself and giving yourself permission to live your life in the way that feels good for you, at a soul level. It doesn't have to be some grand showcase. You don't have to travel for a full year to be happy, or climb Mount Everest or see all Seven Wonders of the World to be fulfilled. If these are dreams of yours, by all means go for it, but true fulfillment isn't in the things you do or achieve, our outward chases. Those will never be enough; we will keep seeking, looking, wanting more; we will never feel satiated, for all of these are external things. Our true joy is not in any one thing. It's in us as we are now. And when we allow ourselves to be where we are, as we are, we can celebrate our life for what it really is— a magnificent, glorious gift. A life well lived is a life of connection. Feeling deeply connected to who you are, what you do, and the people around you is the highest form of joy.

There is no need to chase anything, for everything you need is right here.

You do this when you see that you are the love.

You no longer chase happiness, for you are it.

So it seems the real Joy Seeker is your heart. There was never anything to seek outside of ourselves, but we had to go on this mission to discover what was there all along.

It's simply the language of your own heart.

You are the joy already.

You no longer seek out giant adventures, because your
  life becomes the grand adventure.

You no longer fear the future, for you are one with the
  Universe and your future is now.

You know everything always works out perfectly, and
  life is an unfolding dance that you are actively
  participating in.

To go forth into the great big unknown means you give yourself

- Permission to follow your heart.
- Permission to change your mind.
- Permission to be happy and choose joy.
- Permission to be who you are as you are.
- Permission to flow with the waves of life.
- Permission to have fun and play.
- Permission to be fully present in this moment, for this moment is all there truly is.

The joy we seek is not outside of us. It never was. It was inside you all along.

For everything you have been, everything you are, and everything you will be is fulfillment. Your true self is expressed fully in the world. Go forth, beautiful one, you are everything you need to be, and you are the hero of your own life.

Shine on Joy Seeker.

Shine on.

Manifesto
For Joy Seekers

- MAY YOU HAVE THE COURAGE TO BE TRUE TO YOURSELF AND FOLLOW THROUGH ON YOUR DEEPEST DESIRES.
- DON'T BE AFRAID TO GO AFTER WHAT YOU TRULY WANT, FOR IT'S PART OF YOUR POTENTIAL.
- DON'T BE AFRAID TO CHANGE COURSE, TO CANCEL PLANS, TO MOVE WHERE THE MOVEMENT WITHIN YOU IS LEADING.
- DON'T SETTLE. YOUR LIFE IS FAR TOO PRECIOUS AND GRAND TO HIDE YOUR LIGHT.
- DON'T BE SURPRISED AT HOW FAST THE UNIVERSE WILL MOVE WITH YOU ONCE YOU MAKE A CHOICE.
- DON'T FALL INTO FEAR. IT'S ALL AN ILLUSION. LET YOUR LIGHT AND LOVE MOVE YOU FORWARD.
- IF YOU HAVE TO SACRIFICE WHO YOU ARE AND WHAT MATTERS MOST TO YOU, IT ISN'T WORTH IT.
- YOU ARE WORTH SO MUCH MORE THAN YOU ARE GIVING YOURSELF CREDIT FOR.
- YOU ARE SOURCE ENERGY, LOVE AND LIGHT—NEVER FORGET HOW BEAUTIFUL YOU ARE.
- YOUR HEART IS LOVE AND IT WILL NEVER LEAD YOU ASTRAY.
- HOME IS WHERE YOUR HEART IS, AND YOUR HEART IS WITHIN YOU.

Shine Your Gorgeous Light Free Gift:
Download the Joy Seeker audio
meditation for FREE by visiting

www.playwiththeworld.com/joyseekermeditation

Resources

Notes

Shawn Achor's Ted Talk "The Happy Secret to Better Work"

"The Real Reason You Feel Too Overwhelmed to Work on Your
   Goals" by Mastin Kipp

www.mindbodygreen.com/articles/how-to-achieve-your-goals
   -emotional-trauma

"5 (Doable) Ways to Increase the Love in Your Life" by Brené
   Brown

www.oprah.com/omagazine/how-to-increase-the-love-in-your
   -life-brene-brown/all

Top five regrets of the dying: www.theguardian.com/lifeand
   style/2012/feb/01/top-five-regrets-of-the-dying

Books Referenced

The Power of Meaning: Finding Fulfillment in a World Obsessed with Happiness by Emily Smith

My Friend Fear by Meera Lee Patel

The Tiny Buddha's Worry Journal: A Creative Way to Let Go of Anxiety and Find Peace by Lori Deschene

Mind Over Medicine: Scientific Proof That You Can Heal Yourself by Lissa Rankin

Crazy Sexy Cancer Survivor: More Rebellion and Fire for Your Healing Journey by Kris Carr

You Can Heal Yourself by Louise Hay

The Secret by Rhonda Byrne

You Are a Badass®: How to Stop Doubting Your Greatness and Start Living an Awesome Life by Jen Sincero

The Astonishing Power of Emotions: Let Your Feelings Be Your Guide (Law of Attraction Book 4) by Esther and Jerry Hicks

The Teachings of Abraham by Esther and Jerry Hicks

The Cellars and Ceilings of Summer: An Autobiography of Trance Medium Summer by Summer Bacon

The Book of Mastery: The Mastery Trilogy: Book I by Paul Selig

Big Magic: Creative Living Beyond Fear by Elizabeth Gilbert

The Alchemist by Paulo Coelho

The Desire Map, A Guide to Creating Goals with Soul by Danielle LaPorte

My Go-To List: Books That Radically Transformed My Life

If you want to go deeper into fulfillment and personal growth, these books, authors, and teachers radically impacted my own journey. These are my all-time favorite books and ones I return to again and again for the self-awareness and authentic living.

ESTHER AND JERRY HICKS
The Teachings of Abraham
Ask and It Is Given: Learning to Manifest Your Desires

As you can tell with my references throughout the book, Abraham and Esther Hicks are huge influences on me and my work. This book is part teaching and part to-do and an excellent starter book into the Law of Attraction and manifesting your ideal life.

The Teachings of Kryon by Lee Carroll
The Human Soul Revealed: Unlocking the Mysteries from Beyond by Monika Muranyi Kron

Have you ever wondered about the true nature of the soul, about the role it has in your life and how souls are aspects of a unifying higher consciousness? If so, where is it and how does it function? The answers to these questions and more are given in this book. This book was so instrumental for me healing my insecurities and self-doubt. It's a little heady and scientific at times, but when you tap into the essence of the teaching, the book will flow.

SUMMER BACON AND THE TEACHINGS OF DR. JAMES MARTIN PEEBLES

This School Called Planet Earth

Without a doubt the most powerful teachers for my own growth have been the messages of Dr. Peebles and Summer Bacon. Their teaching is one of love. Through this book we learn why we are here, what we are made for, and how we can make the most of our time on earth.

SANAYA ROMAN AND THE TEACHINGS OF ORIN

Living with Joy: Keys to Personal Power & Spiritual Transformation
Spiritual Growth: Being Your Higher Self

Orin's teachings have profoundly impacted me on my own journey and are the foundation for most of my work. *Spiritual Growth* gives you tools to lift the veils of illusion, see truth, expand and contract time, raise your vibration, achieve higher states of consciousness, open your heart, and know yourself in new, more loving ways. It contains the essence of the contemporary spiritual path, embodying joy, growth, and increased aliveness.

PAUL SELIG AND THE TEACHINGS OF THE GUIDES
The Book of Mastery: The Mastery Trilogy: Book I
The Book of Truth: The Mastery Trilogy: Book II
The Book of Freedom: The Mastery Trilogy: Book III

These books, by far, are the most advanced in concepts and may take a while to fully understand and digest (at least they did for me). But they are great for spiritual advancement and personal soul growth, as they can give you more understanding into your true purpose and reason for being.

Retreats and Wellness Centers

Taking retreats and time out for ourselves is so important for reconnection to our true self. I participated in these programs and have experienced firsthand the healing power.

RYTHMIA LIFE ADVANCEMENT CENTER IN COSTA RICA

Famous for herbal medicine journeys, life coaching programs, and spa treatments. The entire week is dedicated to you diving deep into your purpose and reason for being. A soul seeker's utopia. www.rythmia.com

FAIRMONT CHATEAU LAKE LOUISE, ALBERTA CANADA WELLNESS PROGRAMS

Yearly wellness focused programs including my annual Fall in Love with Yourself and Life retreat and Authentic Living spring retreat. Daily yoga, nature walks, mindful meditation, and workshops. Escape to one of the most breathtaking places in the world to rejuvenate your mind and soul. Lake Louise is a hamlet in Banff National Park in the Canadian Rockies, known for its turquoise, glacier-fed lake, a Unesco World Heritage site. And often said the resting place of Archangel Michael. www.lakelouisewellness.com

FIVELEMENTS IN BALI, INDONESIA

An award winning eco-conscious luxury wellness resort and spa, rooted in principles of raw vegan cuisine, and sacred rituals and arts of the baleens culture. fivelements.org.

To work with the author for speaking and coaching opportunities contact

Shannon@playwiththeworld.com

CONNECT WITH THE AUTHOR
Website: PlayWithTheWorld.com
Facebook: ShannonKaiserWrites
Instagram: ShannonKaiserWrites
Twitter: ShannonLKaiser

Big Hugs and Thanks

Thank you, Steve Harrison and Michele Martin, for believing in me in the very beginning of my writing career and continuing to support all my writing dreams. This book is possible because of you. Thank you, Denise Silvestro, for your enthusiastic partnership and love for me and this work. It is a dream to work with you again. Thank you to the entire Kensington team; thank you for trusting Denise and for helping me get this gorgeous book and message out into the world.

All my mentors along the journey including Summer Bacon and Dr. Peebles, thanks for your unwavering support. And God, my universal support, and Angels, thank you for all of this. Thank you, family, Mom, Dad, Clint, and Rhonda, I love you. And to my close friends, Marita, and Amy, thank you for the behind the scenes support. Francisco Pagán, Jen Dinh, Jordan Aftanas, Talia Pollock and Kate Snowise, you have a special place in my heart and inspire me with your enthusiastic pursuit of turning your dreams into reality.

A huge thanks to my online community: Instagram, Facebook, and Twitter friends, newsletter subscribers, YouTube watchers, and website blog readers. My life coaching and mentorship clients, retreat participants, live workshop and in-person event attendees: This book would not be here without your support, love, and consistent dedication to your own personal growth. You inspire me daily.

And last but not least, a huge big heartfelt thank-you to you, dear reader, for making it this far into the journey and showing up for yourself. Your true Joy Seeker Journey has just begun. Welcome to your beautiful, gorgeous, authentic life.

Connect with Us

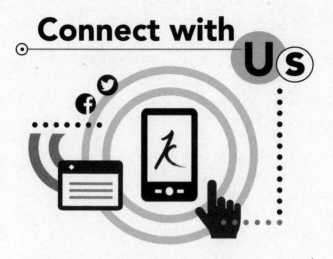

Visit us online at
KensingtonBooks.com
to read more from your favorite authors, see books
by series, view reading group guides, and more.

for sneak peeks, chances to win books and prize packs,
and to share your thoughts with other readers.

facebook.com/kensingtonpublishing
twitter.com/kensingtonbooks

Tell us what you think!

To share your thoughts, submit a review,
or sign up for our eNewsletters, please visit:
KensingtonBooks.com/TellUs.